To Juanita —

Keep laughing —

D0066767

What Mom
Really
Taught Us

Mark Mayfield

Mom's Rules
What Mom Really Taught Us

by Mark Mayfield

Copyright © 2000 by Mark Mayfield
Revised 2011

All rights reserved.
No part of this book may be used or reproduced in any
manner whatsoever without written permission from the
publisher, except in the case of quotations.

Cover Design and Page Layout: Ad Graphics, Tulsa, OK
Cover Photograph: Jeff Kent Bixler
Illustrations : Erick Warner
Printed in the United States of America

ISBN (10 digit): 0-9700349-0-3
ISBN (13 digit): 978-0-9700349-0-8

www.markmayfield.com

Dedication

To my daughters, Leah Christine and Lindsay Michelle. You are the reason I wake up every morning. If you two have had half as much fun being my kids as I have had being your Dad, then I guess I've had twice as much fun as you two . . . if I've done the math correctly. You two remind me everyday that anyone can be a father, but it's really special when you get to be a Dad. I love you both more than hot fudge sundaes.

Table of Contents

Acknowledgments

I'd like to thank the following very smart, kind, patient, creative, and underpaid people for their help in putting this effort together. Evangeline Ysmael, editor extraordinaire; Erick Warner, artist avant-garde; and John McBride, comic connoisseur.

Aren't you tired of over-hyped quotes about somebody's book? Wouldn't you like real quotes from real people? Well here they are. You don't know any of these people. They don't know you. They're just normal people saying normal things about someone who writes a book.

"Big deal, you wrote a book. What do you want . . .a medal?"
— **Sid Simpson**

"I had no idea you were literate."
— **Steve Wyman**

"Everyone knows you're just trying to get in good with your Mom."
— **Don Perkins**

"Do you have a cliff notes version? I don't read anything thicker than a comic book."
— **John Marquardt**

"I hope you make a lot of money on your book. You still owe me four dollars from a golf bet."
— **Mark Horstmann**

"I thought this was going to be a coloring book."
— **Larry Firkins**

"Is this the best you could do?"
— **Jim Booker**

"It's about time you finished this thing."
— **Mom**

My sincere thanks to everyone who took the time to write these deep heartfelt testimonials.

Mom's Rules: What Mom Really Taught Us

My Mom is cool. I want to be clear on that point. There were times when I was young I wasn't so sure, but as the saying goes, as I got older, *she* got smarter. Her rules weren't too restrictive or unfair and some were spoken and some were not. The rules not spoken were the ones that came with the greatest consequences if violated, because "you should have known better, I raised you better than that."

Mom had a foundation for making and/or enforcing rules. "As long as you're living under my roof then you'll live by my rules." She had a very strong negotiating position. Food and shelter are good bargaining chips to have in your corner.

A funny thing happened on the way to adulthood, I became my mother — except for the gender part. What started out as rules for childhood became rules for life. Those rules I was forced to live by, some of which I detested, are the rules I live by today. Those rules weren't just about running in the house or cleaning your plate. They had a much bigger application than that. Painted with a broad brush they make great analogies to live by at home and at work. They taught me how to live, how to function in society, how to cope, and how to be responsible.

I make no pretenses with this book. There is nothing in here you haven't read or heard before. Let's get real, reading this book is not going to change your life. If reading this book could change your life, you're extremely naive or I'm much smarter than I could possibly imagine. This book is to remind you of virtues and values we sometimes overlook. It's common sense but not always common practice. Mom won't remember saying some of these rules, because some were expressed by her body language. A roll of the eyes or a scrunched up forehead at some of our actions clearly made points as to whether a particular behavior was acceptable.

This book is not meant to take anything away from my Dad. He was the greatest man I ever knew and ever will know, whose life was cut short at 48 years. I can only aspire to be the quality of man he was. But my parents had a simple arrangement: Mom made the rules, Dad enforced them. Not all households are like that, but it worked for my Mom and Dad.

I've heard you can measure your contribution on Earth by performing a simple test: Place your finger into a glass of water and then remove it. The size of hole left in the water is the size of your contribution on Earth and how much you will be missed. I'm convinced that if my Mom performed this test, her finger would leave a gaping hole.

This book is an appreciation of what my parents taught me — specifically Mom. She taught me a lot — for starters she taught me how to dress myself and she potty trained me. Those are really handy skills to have, particularly if you ever go out in public. But those are in no way the most significant lessons I learned from her. I learned how to be an asset rather than a liability. I learned we are all one or the other. In the big picture, this may be our best assessment of worth. Do we contribute to society or do we extract from it? In general, this is what I learned from my Mom. Specifically, I learned a bunch of rules that you probably heard as a kid, I just heard a lot more.

Thanks, Ma!

Chapter 1

Get Your Elbows Off The Table

••••••••••••••••••••••••••
Civility
••••••••••••••••••••••••••

When I was a kid growing up in Caney, Kansas, I can remember going to the cafe. We only had one in town and it was a cafe, not a restaurant. The difference between the two was that in addition to eating, a cafe was where you went to drink coffee and solve the world's problems, which could have been anything from the Cuban Missile Crisis to who was going to be Santa Claus in the Christmas parade. One of the first times I went to the cafe, I had both elbows on the table and my head in my hands. I wasn't paying any attention and didn't realize I had each elbow in an empty dinner roll plate. I was using the plates as elbow coasters. That's the first time I recall Mom saying, "Get your elbows off the table."

Now I never questioned Mom that much, but this rule didn't make sense to me. I wasn't hurting anyone, infringing on anyone's rights, being unsafe, or irresponsible. So what was the big deal? Well the big deal was civility. Mom was teaching me civility, the art of grace and class. Other than that opposable thumb, it may be the biggest difference between us and Bonzo (Google that 1950's reference).

With us kids, Mom had to start with the most basic levels, not what fork to use, but that we should be using a fork in the first place. And what about the proper way to eat soup? I won't even describe what we did before we discovered spoons. I wasn't the most uncouth kid at the dinner table though. Sure, I remember having my elbows on the table, the right one was next to my brother's feet. Mom had a real incentive to teach table manners to my brother and me because if she could convince us a spoon was for soup and cereal, we'd stop using it as a launching pad for peas. Come on, I bet you did it too, put some peas in that wonderfully flexible stainless steel spoon, bend it back, and bombs away! Five points for a direct hit on your brother's head and two points for bouncing it off the butter dish. These were manners we learned from the school cafeteria. You remember the food fight in the movie "Animal House"? Our cafeteria made that look like a White House State dinner.

Every time I get on a plane I wonder where civility has gone. Being civil on an airplane means you don't get upset when your bag, which is about one-third the size of the engine, doesn't fit in the overhead compartment. How you got it past the gate in the first place is beyond me. What did you say was in it, something you needed for your health? Like your doctor? How about being civil as we get off the plane? Go ahead, jump up like a jack-in-the-box the minute the wheels hit the runway. Oh, you've retrieved your Samsonite-that-sleeps-six from the overhead compartment without dropping it on my head, but it won't get the plane to the gate a second earlier. I'm not sure, but I don't believe in the history of air travel there has ever been a passenger that beat the plane to the gate. Before saying anything further about civility and behavior on board airplanes, just remember that to the vast majority of passengers, flying isn't a whole lot of fun. An airplane is no longer an exciting, prestigious way to travel. It's a flying freight car. A sardine can in the sky. In fact, if airline seats get any smaller the guy next to you won't just be sharing your space, he'll probably be sharing your lap.

Remember when travel meant looking your best? Not any more. I'm not suggesting we have to dress to the nines, but at least **bathe**. Some people get on the plane looking like they made a snap decision between flying and cleaning out the gutters. They're filthy and they smell. They should have to pay a "smelly surcharge." If you're snapping heads as you walk by, you pay the surcharge. If your five-day deodorant is conking out at noon, you pay the surcharge. If you walk by a goat and his eyes water, you pay the surcharge. The money collected could go toward cleaning up our environment or some other appropriate cause.

Mom always told me that cleanliness was next to godliness. Of course, at the age of ten, I found cleanliness was next to impossible. "You're lucky you're too big for the Maytag," she'd tell me and my brother. I'm not saying Mom was a cleanliness fanatic, but she was close. She once wrote Procter and Gamble asking if "Mr. Clean" made house calls. You could likely catch Mom waxing the vacuum cleaner or ironing socks.

Some people have a different view of cleanliness. They just see the bathtub as a piece of exercise equipment. Pull the plug and fight the current. They obviously don't use it for bathing. How they stand themselves, I don't know. And why do these people always end up next to me in a crowded place? I want to hold up a sign that says, "What you smell is not me, it's him!" And while we're talking about manners in crowded places, how about letting all of us off the elevator before you charge onto it. In the twenty seconds it takes for you to let us off your dentist won't move out of the building, trust me.

And what about those pea brains who enjoy hearing themselves talk so much they talk loud enough for everyone to hear. Someone please tell them that not everything in life is an interesting anecdote. Stop commenting about everything, and when you do comment, keep it below 80 decibels. Here's a news flash for you: Most of the world doesn't think you're as interesting as you do.

Politeness needs a comeback. Opening a door, offering a chair, putting trash where it belongs, cleaning up after yourself, and other civil acts have merit. Yes, it can be frustrating to pass those good, handicapped parking spots. What are the odds that six handicapped people are going to arrive all at the same time? But pass them by and instead of grumbling that you have to walk so far, be grateful you can.

Here's another civility check. When you're in a supermarket checkout line and your basket is holding enough food for the population of Peoria, do you let that guy with just a gallon of milk go ahead of you? I hope so. Ralph Waldo Emerson wrote, "Life is not so short but that there is always time for courtesy." Remember, to be born a gentleman is an accident, but to die one is an achievement. I figured out in my short life that civility and good deeds make one feel really good. And in case you didn't know, that is the great desire of all human beings — to feel good. Why do you think there are so many massage therapists?

This may sound like I'm advocating a very high-society, stuffy, prim and proper order. NO WAY! Anyone who knows me will verify that I'm about as earthy as they come. I would just like to see a bit more decency and civility in our lives. So here are some civility hints:

1) If you've been wearing those jeans for a week…wash them.

2) If you smell like Hulk Hogan's locker…take a shower.

3) If your office looks like a tornado hit it…organize it.

4) If you wear brown a lot because it goes with your yellow teeth…buy a toothbrush.

5) If you found a nest of rabbits in your car…clean it out.

6) If you've been sitting 20 minutes at the restaurant and nobody has taken your order…there must be a reason. You've probably got your elbows on the table.

Chapter 2

Straighten Up Or You're Going To Bed

Choices

"Straighten up or you're going to bed!" Mom threw this ominous threat at us constantly. Going to bed was bad; going to bed early was tragic. Staying up is what kids live for. The later a kid gets to stay up the better day he has. Making matters worse in this "early-to-bed" issue was the bogie man, who lives in the bedroom. The only room where he lives — despite what anybody says. Fortunately, keeping the blanket over your head protected you from him. I'm not sure how this worked exactly. The bogie man possessed great strength and performed Herculean feats, but he could not pull the blanket off your head. Must have been some severe allergy to wool or fabrics in general. Much like the Superman-kryptonite thing.

I always wanted to stay up later than what my parents thought was appropriate. This was fairly normal for kids. I would whine, beg, and plead for just another half hour so I could watch a show like "Bonanza," which, for you Generation X-ers, was a popular, long-running western show that was way before its time. It featured a single parent raising sons with politically incorrect names like, Little Joe and Hoss. "Bonanza" was about three men in their forties who still lived with their "Paw," and every time one of them fell in love, the young lady would fall into a well and die. Or she'd be struck by lightning or get a fatal disease. In fact, as a kid I would yell at the TV when I saw a woman starting to fall for one of these guys. "Don't do it Miss Molly. Leave him, run for your life."

What I'm saying is, not going to bed was a reward, a treat. Conversely, going to bed early was a punishment. Humiliating punishment. If your siblings got to stay up while you were sent to bed, you knew you were in for some real hassling when they finally came to bed. They would tell you about the great shows they watched, the ice cream they had, the games they played, the amusement parks they visited. You get the point. This was just another way that your parents could humiliate you. Parents are innately good at humiliating their kids. This metamorphosis apparently occurs at conception and lasts their entire lives.

"Mom, I'm 16. I don't want the Barney lunch box anymore."

And Dads could always find a way to embarrass their kids — like wearing their trousers higher as they got older. By the time Dads are 60, most of them have to unbuckle their pants just to brush their teeth. This is why kids, when they traveled with their parents often wore camouflage gear, so they could conceal themselves by hiding in the back seats and running undercover. "Dad, when you take me over to Tommy's house, could you drop me off, like, about six blocks from his house. And, if you don't mind, I'm going to crouch in this back seat on the way over."

When your friends came over, you would encourage Dad to not tell any of the old corny jokes and not to wear that stupid-looking flowered shirt, and if "you wouldn't mind maybe you could watch TV down in the basement."

Yes, parents humiliate their kids, it's one of the laws of the jungle and going to bed early was one of those humiliating experiences. I've often wondered, if you really were tired as a kid, would going to bed early be a punishment? How would you punish somebody who was really tired? "Okay, tonight you've got to stay up late. That's right, you're going to watch the The Learning Channel on compound adjectives. And after that, you're going to watch Martha Stewart make seven different Christmas gifts out of Ziplock bags. And, when that's over, you're going to stay up and visit with Uncle Leo, who's bringing over the slides from his trip to Toledo." But that probably wouldn't happen as a kid, because kids live to stay up late, which is exactly the opposite of adults. Adults wouldn't see going to bed early as punishment. It would be a reward, because we're exhausted. "You went to bed at 9:00 o'clock last night? You bragger."

As kids, it's a different story. Mom knew that being sent to bed was real punishment, so she doled it out when all else failed. She placed the decision in our hands. We were allowed to decide what was going to happen. It all rested on that little word, "or." "Straighten up, *or*, you're going to bed." You decide. You make the call.

We get these options all the time in life. Take care of your car with regular maintenance, *or* pay high repair bills in a couple of years. Eat right and exercise, *or* experience premature health problems. Take care of your employees, *or* they're going to leave. Fix Social Security, *or* the next generation won't have it.

Choosing options is a tough decision-making responsibility. And it's probably tougher today than ever before because we have so many options. When did we start having all of these options? I bet a caveman didn't have all those options. He didn't say, "Og, these are nice wooden clubs you've got there, could I have one. Not the maple, could you give me one in oak?" Or pioneers who settled the West probably never had conversations like, "Look Betsy, I bought a new covered wagon, but this one didn't have the fold-down rear seat, and I'm not very happy with it."

Today, we've got a zillion options. Do we really need extra hot Tabasco sauce? Who eats this stuff? People with lead lips? How about Imodium Advanced and Imodium AD. The only difference between these two products is that Imodium AD is faster acting. I'm wondering: Who would not want the faster acting Imodium?

Garbage bags now come in more than one color. What are we supposed to match with our trash bags? More of that Martha Stewart influence, I suppose.

I labor over buying athletic shoes today, because there are just so many options. Running shoes, or cross-training shoes, or work-out shoes, or court shoes, or sneakers? Or the ultimate in shoe redundancy, walking shoes. Are there some shoes *not* recommended for walking?

I get puzzled by all of the hair spray options, as well. Which really is the better holding hair spray? Ultra hold, super hold, deluxe hold, or maximum hold? I just want the hair spray that is made to really hold — the one made from the same stuff they use to cover gymnasium floors.

Making decisions is not always easy, but at least we can be thankful we have choices to make. Yet we often shrink from that decision-making responsibility. Not making a choice, in itself is a choice. The sad thing is often life will present us with a choice of evils rather than a choice of goods. Making the choice is the hard part. It doesn't take much strength to do things, but it takes a lot of strength to decide what things to do.

Remember as a small child when you had to decide how you were going to have that first loose tooth removed? Were you going to pull it yourself? Would you have your father pull it, or were you going to have it removed by gravity? Choices, choices, choices. Making a decision may be the most difficult step in the problem-solving process, but it can't be avoided. The difference between the have's and the have not's is often traced back to the did's and the did not's. Nothing ever gets done unless there is a conscious decision to do it. How's that for profound redundancy?

We need to make choices and we need to make better choices. We need to forget small faults and remember little kindnesses. We need to condemn less and commend more. We need to use things and love people, not love things and use people.

So the next time you're faced with this or that. Good or bad. Right or wrong, make a choice. Wake up. Stand up. Straighten up, or you're going to bed.

Chapter 3

Nobody Likes A Bragger

Modesty

A quick way to catch Mom's wrath was to increase your level of cockiness or bravado. You'd be sure to hear, "Nobody likes a bragger." She instilled in us that "you tell yourself you're the best; but let other people tell the world." Modesty is the art of encouraging people to find out how important you are. You're not supposed to tell them. That would take the fun out of it. Let them find out on their own. Modesty and its opposite, arrogance, are the easiest traits to see in a person. Make sure they see modesty. When we think we know it all, we don't. In other words, the head never begins to swell until the mind stops growing.

Our family was very modest and we believed the old saying, "We're modest because we've got lots to be modest about." Another reason our heads never swelled was because we made fun of ourselves and, trust me, we had lots of material. I once was buying slacks in a very nice clothing store in Washington, D.C. when I decided to see if there was another style in my size. I found them on the rack and then changed right in the middle of the store without thinking. I had a complete mental shut down. Have you ever tried to act nonchalant wearing only a shirt, boxers, and shoes in a busy department store? There are several ways to handle the situation. Walk quickly over to alterations and say in a loud voice, "You said my pants would be ready an hour ago." Or, you can tilt your head at that strange angle and go into your mannequin impression. Or you can just squat in a Yoga position, close your eyes, and begin humming. I chose the latter.

Another time I was checking out of a grocery store standing behind a lady wearing perhaps the world's worst wig. It looked like a throw rug from a hamster cage. On top of its unfortunate quality, the wig was crooked. I don't know what I could have been thinking — but I straightened it. She did not appreciate my concern for her appearance. Straightening a person's wig in public will not bring you lots of gratitude. It ranks right up there with telling a guy, "Your bald spot is showing." This is how my family kept our egos in check. These brainless imperfections are what makes all of us normal.

No one is perfect, so no one has the right to boast and brag as if they are. Here's another example. I like to think I am a fairly intelligent person, but when I bought my first cordless telephone, my neighbor convinced me that I had to point the antenna in the direction of the party to whom I was speaking. This meant, of course, that when I called somebody

I often ended up saying things like, "Mom, you're starting to fade, are you proceeding in a south by southeast direction?" I had been doing this for about a month when my neighbor noticed me tilting my head awkwardly while on the phone. He informed me he had only been kidding. We still laugh about it. Ego back in check!

Much of the time, modesty disappears because we are trying to be *cool*. Or, we're trying to "keep up with the Joneses." Our competitive fires take over and we engage in the one-upmanship game. Before you know it, arrogance has taken over and we're strutting like peacocks thinking we're better than everyone else. This all started because we had to be *cool*. I used to watch my neighbor take his dog for a walk in the evening. I was envious of how macho he looked as he and his German Shepherd pranced down the street. I wanted to be that cool, but I only had a cat. I decided I would be cool if I taught my cat to go for a walk. I bought a red kitty collar and leash and prepared to take him for a walk. As soon as I attached the leash he laid on the ground like a brick. I'd pick him up and he would just lie back down. I decided he just needed a little encouragement. So I started to gently tug on the leash. He then stood up and with his front paws braced himself against my pulling. It was now a battle. A crowd had gathered and they were saying, "Are you taking your cat for a drag?" I responded "No, I'm just declawing him." After a futile hour, it became evident the cat's will was stronger than mine. This wasted time and effort was solely because I wanted to look *cool*. I wanted attention. I needed my ego stroked.

Not too many people can get away with displaying a big ego. The great baseball player of the 1930s and later a TV announcer in the '60s, Dizzy Dean, could. He used to say, "It ain't braggin' if you can do it." That may have worked for old Diz' but it won't for most of us. This is why I like self-effacing flight attendants, store clerks, government officials, etc. They've learned the first rule in getting along with the public is to take their jobs seriously, but aren't quite so intense about how seriously they take themselves. Good speakers know this. One of the best ways to get an audience on your side is to tell a joke, and the best joke you can tell is one on yourself.

We are all imperfect. It's a trait we all have in common. We all do goofy stuff. If you don't believe me, what do you say when you call someone at three in the morning arousing them from a dead sleep? "Did I wake you? Were you sleeping?" They often offer a brilliant response like, "No, I was just lying down. I've been lying down for six hours now." These are the moments of stupidity that should soften your ego and cool that "I'm-the-greatest" mentality.

Nobody is the greatest! That guy died a couple of thousand years ago. I get so irked when I see athletes pumping their fists, screaming, strutting, dancing, and belittling their opponents after they've made a play. Half the time, they're still behind! It's like rolling in a 40-foot putt for a triple bogey . . . big deal! Real winners don't do that showboat stuff. They give their opponents due respect, tell them "great effort," and hand the ball to the official. Modesty and sportsmanship are nearly synonymous, and both traits are nearly extinct. One of the reasons everybody thinks Michael Jordan was the greatest basketball player ever is because he never said he was. He just went out and did his job. Notice anything there? Remember that a person wrapped up in himself makes a very small package. So the next time you slam dunk over me, or pick a better mutual fund, or buy a cooler car, don't rub it in my face. Just pat me on the rump and say, "Good effort." Because nobody likes a bragger. My Mom says so.

Chapter 4

You're Not The Only One At The Table

· ·

Philanthropy

· ·

Eating at the dinner table with my family was akin to watching wild hyenas fighting over a recent kill. We ate like wild animals. If we'd ever invited Marlin Perkins to dinner, he would have come with a whip and a tranquilizer gun. We took no prisoners at the dinner table. Imagine Sherman's march through Georgia done with a knife and a fork. If you waited around you were likely to starve to death. We were nothing more than a pack of hyenas. This was primarily a survival skill that even Mom understood. Heck, she was in there scraping with the rest of us. You have to wonder, what do hyena mothers say when their meals get wild and woolly? Something like, "Now stop it! All of you! You're acting like a bunch of wild Mayfields."

Mom never used the hyena comparison. She would often accuse us of "acting like a bunch of monkeys." Which was technically incorrect — we never ended dinner by swinging from room to room on the light fixtures, except for that one time my brother had too many sugar cookies.

I was always amazed our dining habits didn't lead to food fights or even an accidental fork stuck in the back of your hand as you reached for that second sweet roll. All I have are a few fingernail-scrape scars. I think everyone understood that a fight would just take you away from the feast, and then both of you would lose out. Come to think of it, when I watched those hyenas eating their wild game, they never fought — they growled and snapped at one another, but they were not going to get in a tussle because even if they emerged the victor, they would find what they were fighting for was gone.

I'm convinced our family genetics include some hyena heritage. Occasionally, we would cross the line and become too hyena-like and Mom would shout, "Hey, you're not the only one at the table!" Mom wanted us to realize the world is full of givers and takers and you are either one or the other. While we all know that you have to watch out for Numero Uno, Mom wanted us to watch out for others. It was Mom's first lesson in philanthropy. She never used the word philanthropy because we wouldn't understand it and she had trouble spelling it, but we could grasp and spell the concept of giving and taking. Giving isn't a once-a-year Christmas thing and it's not necessarily material gifts. More often than not it means giving a helping hand or giving your time or giving another intangible like caring.

I blew an engine belt on my car driving through Iowa sometime back and was forced to limp into a gas station that, fortunately, did minor engine repair. Unfortunately though, they didn't have that belt in stock and needed to get it at an auto parts store, but it was early in the morning and none were open yet. I was in a time jam and really couldn't wait the two hours for the stores to open. That's when I saw the mechanic walking toward his own vehicle with his tools in hand. I asked him what he was up to and he said, "The belt size you need is exactly like the one on my car. So I'll take it off of my car and put it on yours." I then began looking for a full eclipse, an easy Double Jeopardy answer, peppy elevator music, or some other rare occurrence. I'd never seen a mechanic perform such an act of philanthropy (there's that word again). Most mechanics aren't any different than the rest of us: "I'm going to keep my stuff and I'm not going to give any of it to you." This mechanic was an exception, he was a real giver.

Imagine if everyone was like that Iowa mechanic. You would go into your bank and ask for a loan and your banker would pull out his wallet. Your furnace would quit and the repairman would loan you blankets until he could get the parts for repair. You need a kidney transplant and your surgeon would cut open his, well . . . you see where I'm going with this. There's only one way to teach giving and it's by example. I can almost guarantee that if your kids don't see the qualities of care and generosity in you, you won't see it in them.

I learned giving from the women in my family. My Grandma was from the old school. She had those old school words like: gallivantin' and caddywampus. Grandma was also from the old school of giving. She never was wealthy, but always was giving things away: cookies, eggs, kittens, homemade preserves, canned pickles, Grandpa... Grandma was a giver, not a taker. My sister, Gina, is a carbon copy of her. Everyone else's welfare is more important to her than her own. When she says, "How ya doin'?" she really means it. She believes the takers may eat better, but the givers sleep better. And so she gives. She gives to her kids, to all her family, to her friends, to her church. She is the personification of the verse, "It is more blessed to give than to receive." She most often gives a gift you can't wrap and you can't buy. She gives her heart . . . she gives her time. So which are you — a giver or a taker?

Bob Hope was known to say, "If you haven't got any charity in your heart, you have the worst kind of heart trouble." We all need to have a more volunteer, charitable attitude. We need to be philanthropists (I love that word). It was Victor Hugo who said, "As the purse is emptied, the heart is filled."

So here's your test of philanthropy: Do you sit on your hands when the civic leader asks for volunteers to help on a Saturday? Do you rush to get the last bit of jelly out of the jar? Do you tell the United Way caller that you can't afford a $10 contribution, then hop in your car to go buy a six-pack and some cigarettes? Do you scoop out that last bit of ice cream for yourself? Do you refuse to answer the phone if the Caller ID shows the Red Cross is calling? Do you race for the end chair at a table, so you can have all the table space possible? Do you? If you do, stop it, you're not the only one at the table.

Chapter 5

Lighten Up, You'll Laugh About That Someday

Laughter

In our family we prefer laughing over crying. Rather than get upset over something, we were encouraged to find the lighter side of the situation. If Mom caught us moping around, she would say, "Lighten up, you'll laugh about this someday." She was right. Those traumatic moments I endured years ago cause belly laughs now. You've probably caught yourself saying, "I'll laugh about this in five years." Why wait? If you're going to laugh eventually — why waste time? Laugh now.

There was a time when my daughters' hobby was totaling cars. One span of three years I bought six cars. My insurance premium looked like a ransom note. In fact, I think my insurance agent named his new boat after one of my daughters. One of the vehicles was wrecked when my oldest daughter, Leah, trying to avoid potholes in the road, veered off the pavement, then turned too sharply to get the car back on the highway. Her car rolled and was totaled, but she walked away from it (she says she ran away from it). We laugh about the incident now, and if you know teenage girls and their cars you know why. My daughters live in their cars. I'm not sure they really need airbags in their cars — not as long as they have their gym bags and four complete changes of clothing next to them on the seat. They also could be stranded in a snow bank for weeks and would survive. In addition to the clothes for all four seasons, there is food in abundance. French fries are on the floor, half-eaten hamburgers and bottles of pop are everywhere. As the car was rolling, shoes were flying out of the car. We found nine shoes on the road. Even though it was nearly tragic, Leah and I laugh about it.

I remember a dinner awards banquet years ago when the gentleman on the far right of the elevated platform at the head table decided to adjust his chair slightly and then slipped off the riser. As he was falling, he grabbed the tablecloth and pulled everyone's half-eaten meal on their laps. They all jumped up, but in doing so, first scooted their chairs back and disappeared off the back of the platform. This all happened in what appeared to be a nanosecond. Poof! Everybody was gone. People were yelling, dishes were breaking, food was everywhere. Reminded me of dinner at one of my family reunions. After order was restored, the first award recipient was a very tall man. He paid no attention as he stepped onto the riser and hit his forehead on a ceiling fan. He covered his wound with his handkerchief as he accepted the award — recognition for working 20 years without time lost due to an accident.

At another event I went to the men's room before going on stage and quite unfortunately, left my fly open as I came back from the banquet room. The meeting planner noticed, and as I sat down he asked if my fly was open. Now this is not what I heard. I had some tight travel connections on my mind and I thought he said "flight" instead of "fly." Here's how the conversation went:

Him: Is your fly open? (I thought he said "flight.")

Me: Sure.

Him: What?

Me: It's always open this time of year.

Him: What?

Me: When it's not busy, you can pretty much count on it being open.

After we realized we were talking about different things, we laughed about it. Laughing gives you distance from problems, and in case you didn't know, it's much easier to solve problems when we have a little distance from them. It's easier when we see the big picture, or a macro perspective rather than a micro perspective.

My inspiration for this is my brother, Elton, who is without a doubt, the funniest man in our family. If he ever decided to ditch his career in advertising and marketing, he could make it as a comedy writer. He's had more than his share of troubles in his life, but always seems to rebound because he laughs about it. He puts things in perspective by making fun of the situation, making fun of himself, and laughing. If you ever need a lift, call him. I guarantee he will make you laugh.

There's not a person in this world who can't laugh. You don't have to be Robin Williams, Whoopi Goldberg, or Bill Cosby because it's not your ability to make other people laugh that is important, it's your ability to laugh — at yourself.

None of us is perfect. Some of us know people who think they are perfect. They usually have an "ex" in their names, like "ex-friend, ex-husband, ex-boss, and so on. The fact that we're not perfect creates a wealth of opportunities to laugh at ourselves. Do you remember the Dean Martin celebrity roasts which were on TV during the '70s and '80s? They were huge ratings successes because everybody likes to laugh at famous people, especially famous people who can laugh along. You may not be rich and famous, but I bet you have as many faults and foibles as anyone else. Here's an exercise for you. Pretend you're writing your own roast. Make a list of the topics you could kid about. Now start poking fun at yourself whenever you can. People will like you for it.

Now I am one big batch of comedic screw ups. I can pretty much guarantee that I've done more goofy stuff than you. In fact, if I had a dime for every silly thing I've ever done, I'd make the Rockefellers look like charity cases. Remember, I'm the only guy that I know who straightened a wig on an unsuspecting lady. When I say that we all can laugh at ourselves, I am first and foremost including myself. Your hipbone may be connected to your knee bone, and your knee bone to your shin bone, but your funny bone is connected to your heart. Those of us who can laugh at ourselves, have the kind of heart that makes friends. If you can't laugh at yourself, you can bet other people are, so you might as well join the crowd.

I'm not saying you just belly laugh all your problems away. It's not going to change the stock market or change the weather, but laughter is like a car's bumper. It can't protect you in the really big collisions, but it can help you survive life's daily fender-benders.

One of the main reasons we need to laugh is to reduce tension in our lives. You can't laugh and be tense at the same time. The scientific verification of this comes from the phrase, "I laughed so hard I wet my pants." You can't wet your pants and be tense; it's impossible. Try going to the bathroom all tensed up. There's no bathroom activity unless you're relaxed. I'm not suggesting you perform an exercise to test this hypothesis, just trust me on this one. Laughter reduces tension. I see this all the time. Recently I was on a plane on which a lady had a heart attack. She was stabilized and moved to the front of the aircraft as we made our descent. After we landed, the flight attendant asked for everyone to remain seated while the paramedics removed their patient from the plane. At that point a passenger became hostile because he thought he might miss a connection. He was shouting at the flight attendants to find some other way off the aircraft. The tension was thick. Then a gentleman in front of me turned, looked at the irate passenger and said, "Excuse me, sir, if I ever have a heart transplant, I want yours. It's obviously never been used." The entire plane erupted in laughter and you could feel the tension leave the plane.

Would the Cold War have been shorter if Khrushchev and Kennedy wore funny hats and told each other jokes? I don't know, but it would have been worth a try. Russians, especially, always seem pretty grim. Come to think of it, if there is an official Russian joke book, it's gotta be pretty thin. You probably know it takes a lot more muscles to frown than it does to smile. I know some of you crabby apples are saying, "They're my muscles and I'll do with them what I want." But the point is there's no reason to give your face a workout. Don't tighten up, lighten up and smile.

You may also be aware of the fact that doctors will tell you laughing is good for you. Endorphins are secreted, blood flow is improved, respiration is enhanced. I believe this is one reason that women live longer than men. Women laugh more than men. There must be some cause and effect here; this can't be just a coincidence. The life expectancy of a woman is about 82 and of a man is approximately 76. Now, men have two options. Either adopt a woman's sense of humor, or at 75 have a sex change. I think we know which will be cheaper and easier.

Laughter and play keeps us young. We don't stop playing because we grow old, we grow old because we stop playing. There have been several best selling books centered around this idea. I know some of the authors of those books, and that idea must be true, because they're laughing all the way to the bank. And how about that phrase: "Laughing all the way to the bank." Taken one way, it generally means pulling a fast one on somebody and making money doing it. I prefer to take it another way — it refers to those authors I mentioned who have made money by giving the world something to enjoy . . . something to laugh about and to help a whole bunch of us to lighten up. If I ever laugh all the way to the bank, I hope it's because a lot of people are laughing with me.

James Matthew Barrie said, "Those who bring sunshine to the lives of others cannot keep it from themselves." So the next time you're getting ready to snap somebody's head off because your order isn't exactly right, or the next time you forgot underwear on a trip and you're washing out your dirty ones in the hotel bathroom sink and drying them with the hair dryer . . . lighten up, you'll laugh about it some day.

Chapter 6

Oh Be Quiet, It Can't Hurt That Much

··························

Coping

··························

W hen I was in my early teens, I was thrown from a horse — landed head-first into a rock-filled ditch, busted open my forehead, and came running into the house screaming. Mom quickly grabbed me and nonchalantly started cleaning the wound. After a few seconds of me sobbing uncontrollably, she startled me by saying, "Oh be quiet, it can't hurt that much." My first thought was child abuse. My second thought was what an insensitive Mom I had. My third thought was I noticed it wasn't hurting anymore. Who knows how long I would have cried without Mom's casual approach.

I think Mom was nonchalant about accidents for two reasons: first, Dad was a walking accident. He wasn't unsafe, just unlucky — he was always bandaged up for some reason. If he had been an electrician, he would have had no eyebrows. For Dad, carrying fingernail clippers was considered being armed and dangerous. He could get hurt in any room in the house.

Mom was around injury all the time, but the main reason for Mom's apparent lack of concern for a small head wound was that she gave birth to six kids. This was before epidurals. This was when they gave the woman a shot of whiskey and a stick to bite on. This was when men never went into the delivery room. And you know why? Because if that woman in labor could've slipped out of those stirrups and gotten her hands on the man responsible, she would have put him in orbit. So when men of my Dad's generation said they didn't go into the delivery room because they didn't want to see pain and suffering, they're referring to their own pain and suffering. But no pain and suffering can compare to childbirth — except possibly a paper cut. From a man's perspective, nothing can equal the pain of a paper cut.

Mom wasn't being insensitive when she told me to be quiet and that it couldn't hurt; she was just trying to teach me to be tough. She wanted all of us kids to be able to cope in a world of whiners. People can't seem to handle anything anymore. We complain and cry about everything. Here are some signs you may be one of those whiners:

1) You can't make it to work because you have a temperature of 98.7.

2) You're so upset after your favorite football team loses that you have to hide the razor blades in your house.

3) You stayed in bed for two days after Ginger left the Spice Girls.

4) You can't eat Rice Krispies because they are too loud.

5) You saw Mister Rogers as aggressive and abrasive.

6) You go to the emergency room to get the lint from your navel removed.

7) You become sullen and withdrawn after losing your library card.

8) You write a letter to the editor protesting the paper's decision to change it's font.

9) You're worried the landlord will decide your goldfish violates his "No Pets" rule.

10) You notice the "Don't Remove This Tag" tag isn't on your mattress, and you have nightmares about search warrants and SWAT teams.

People, get over it! Deal with it. When we pay excessive attention to the little problems and peccadilloes, we blow them completely out of proportion and create more anguish than what they merit. The only way we can develop coping skills is to just simply cope. Prosperity may be a great teacher, but adversity is a greater one. We've all heard that whatever doesn't kill you makes you stronger. Well, that's because it makes us stronger in our minds. Washington Irving said, "Little minds are tamed and subdued by misfortunes, but great minds rise above them."

My daughter Lindsay accompanied me on a trip to Northwest Iowa when she was about 10. About an hour into the trip, my pickup began to overheat (that's right, I have a pickup . . . but I don't have curtains in the back window). It was a Sunday afternoon and nothing was open so all we could do was drive a few miles and then stop and let the engine cool off. Every little town in Northwest Iowa has a golf course, so we started stopping at each course along the way. We would putt and chip for a while and then head to the next town. This could have been an awful trip, but we figured out a way to make it fun. We figured out a way to cope.

When we learn how to cope, we begin to learn how to be happy because doing without some of the things you want is an indispensable part of happiness. Coping with life's adversities is an integral part of being happy; and coping means separating real stress from just plain inconvenience. It helps our mental health to understand the difference. For example, being caught in a traffic jam is inconvenient; getting caught in a traffic jam while your wife counts her contractions is STRESS! Having your boss show up for dinner 30 minutes early is inconvenient; having him show up on Tuesday instead of Wednesday is STRESS! Running into an old girlfriend while you're at the movies with your wife is inconvenient; running into your wife while you're at the movies with your girlfriend is STRESS!

In stress management classes we are taught there are two natural responses: fight or flight. We can fight it by managing it, or we can just run from it. There is, however, a third legitimate option: ignore it. I'm not talking denial here. Say you have a situation in your life that is troubling you and you can't avoid it. Ask yourself if you can do something to fix it or change it. If the answer is no — then just *ignore* it. Forget fight or flight. Just plain forget about it! We need to just ignore some of the pain in life and stop worrying about it. Nobody wants to hear you whine anyway. Most of the people don't care, and the others are glad somebody else is worse off than they are. Outside of your immediate family, most folks who ask how you're doing don't really want to know anyway. Especially when your answer includes a detailed analysis of your last CAT scan.

You've seen the best seller, *Don't Sweat the Small Stuff: And It's All Small Stuff,* by Richard Carlson. Well, it so happens that the author is right. And here's how to tell if what you're worrying about is worth breaking a sweat over: Would it make the evening news? For example, have you ever heard a newscaster say, "This bulletin just in . . . a local man has lost his car keys at the mall, and we've got a crew en route to the scene." I don't think so. Losing your car keys is no big deal. This wouldn't make the news. It's different though, if you've lost your nephew Kevin, who you're supposed to be watching. That is a big deal. So just learn to apply the Evening News Rule and you'll soon be dividing your worries into the trivial and the truly important.

In simple terms, we need to quit bellyaching about everything. Adversity causes some people to break, it causes others to break records. The people who complain about the way the ball bounces are usually the ones that dropped it in the first place. So toughen up. We all encounter inconveniences in our lives, and the more we whine about it, the more it's going to hurt. So just be quiet. It can't hurt that much.

Chapter 7

Get A Mind Of Your Own

Creativity

If there is one thing that Mom hated, it was not thinking. I can still hear her say after one of my bone-head moves, "What were you thinking?" You know what types of things I'm talking about — juggling your little brother's shoes while he's still in them, watching the cat jump back and forth in the spin cycle, or gargling grape Kool Aid while wearing a white shirt. After Mom would shout "What were you thinking?" I would offer a snappy comeback like, "Well, Billy did it." I knew this rationale wouldn't fly. Just because somebody else was stupid enough to do it didn't mean that it was okay for me to do it. I would still try, and Mom would respond with, "Well, if Billy jumped off a bridge, would you have done that too?" Mom would put me in my place by saying, "Will you just get a mind of your own."

Mom hated us kids not thinking. She knew a mind unemployed was a mind unenjoyed. An unemployed mind gets you into trouble because a person is not rewarded for having brains, he is rewarded for using them. Too many of us operate on autopilot. Without using our brain capacity, we are doomed for failure. But we do it all the time, and there is no sadder or more frequent obituary on the pages of time than "we have always done it this way." We are creatures of habit in the purest sense. We do it just because that's the way we've always done it.

Take a look at society and see the uncreative world we live in. I can be lost in a department store, wandering up and down the aisles, moving things off the shelf, when a salesperson says, "Are you looking for something?" I tell them, "No, I'm shoplifting, leave me alone." At a convenience store, I placed six apples on the counter only to hear the clerk say, "Do you want a sack?" I said, "No, give me a stick, I'll roll them home." These people were operating on autopilot. No cerebral activity. And they are not the exception, they are the rule. I see a billboard for illiteracy that says, "For more information, write . . ." When I owned a nightclub, people would call and ask if we had live bands. I said, "No, we have dead ones; tonight it's Patsy Cline and Roy Orbison." And I recently went into a bagel shop and ordered one dozen bagels. The clerk asked if they were "to go." I said, "No, I'm sitting here until I've eaten all twelve of them."

We don't think. Mom hated that. She knew that creativity was what separated the winners from the losers. Often, instead of thinking we blindly follow the leader or just do it out of habit. Well, for heaven's sakes, don't think. You could cause brain burnout. Henry Ford once said, "Thinking is the hardest work in the world, no wonder so few people do it." Maybe this is why I truly admire those who think, those who put their creativity to work and come up with a new idea, product, or service. They weren't satisfied with the status quo. These are the people who thought of light-weight golf bags, fast food breakfast, beer can coolies, refrigerator magnets, and remote controls. These are the people making a difference. These are the people who see opportunity. They understand that sight is a faculty, but seeing is an art. They're creating change, they're thinking out of the box. These individuals' words and actions stay with me.

One summer day I was in my hotel room preparing for an engagement when I realized I had forgotten shoes. Even though I feel I have been traveling my entire life, I still manage to forget items from time to time. I needed to be on stage for a sound check in 15 minutes and I had no shoes. The only shoes I had were the ones I wear when I travel in the summer . . . white loafers. I had on a dark double-breasted suit and white loafers. I looked like a very confused Pat Boone. After unsuccessfully trying to steal, I mean borrow, the bellman's shoes, I asked the front desk if they had any suggestions. They directed me to a clothing store across the street. I didn't have time to go upstairs and change into casual clothes, so I headed into the store wearing my dark suit and white loafers. The owner had just opened. He stopped and stared at me. I looked at him and said, "What do you suppose I need?" Without hesitation, he replied, "A white suit." My first thought was that he was a funny guy. But on further review, I realized he was a *creative* guy. He realized the commission or the profit margin on a suit was much greater than on a pair of shoes. Creativity is the key component in the problem-solving process. Creative people thinking for themselves, getting off autopilot, make the world go round.

I believe with the death of creativity quickly comes death of the entity. So are you creative, or are you on autopilot? When you buy a shovel, do you ask for an owner's manual? Do you volunteer to play piano in the marching band? Do you think ranch dressing has something to do with jeans and western shirts? It's not that hard to avoid brain burnout; it's simple. You exercise your mind. You can do tough problems in your head, like figuring out who's older, Santa Claus or the Tooth Fairy; or memorize significant documents, like the Constitution, the Declaration of Independence, or the theme to Gilligan's Island; or ponder the tragedies of our time, who's responsible for the death of JFK? Who hired Jerry Springer?

Developing your creativity is what sets you apart from all those people set on autopilot. Start to think differently. Why don't you try to patent something that can be worn *and* eaten? Develop a medical exam gown that covers your "assets." How about a beeper that goes off in overdue library books? Or a trap door that opens up automatically in the express lane if a person rolls up with $712 worth of groceries.

We need to get back into the idea business. We need to create ideas — lots of them. Remember, some ideas die because they're sitting in solitary confinement. You can spot those people with no ideas, people who haven't had an original thought since 1981. Their eyes look like they've just been coated with Crisco, and they've got the attention span of a hummingbird. Choose the alternative to this, be creative. Adopt a questioning attitude. Ask the question, "Why?" Why don't they just make airplanes out of the same stuff they make that black box? Why is "abbreviated" such a long word? Why don't sheep shrink when it rains? Open your eyes *and* your mind. Remember, the mind is like a parachute. To work it must be opened. So think for yourself and don't just jump off the bridge because Billy did it. Do it because it was your idea and because it was a good idea.

Turn off the autopilot. Get a mind of your own.

Chapter 8

Always Wear Clean Underwear

••••••••••••••••••••••••

Flexibility

••••••••••••••••••••••••

We all know why Mom wanted us in clean underwear … just in case we were in an accident. We all know what happens to peoples' muscle control in an accident . . . or put another way, "loose lips may sink ships, but a nervous bladder will make the doctors madder."

I wondered if that really meant dirty underwear patients got poor treatment from emergency room personnel. Are they evaluating patients based on a secret DU (Dirty Underwear) code; or does it go beyond that? Are you rated on style, brand,

color, as well as cleanliness of your skivvies? Do red silk thongs speed up medical care? And what if you didn't wear underwear at all? What would happen then? Clean underwear is a narrow possibility anyway. Technically speaking, right after you have them on, they're dirty. So I'm not sure dirty underwear really makes a difference. I've watched those hospital television dramas; I've never heard them say, "I need an IV . . . stat . . . no, wait a minute, he's wearing dirty underwear. I'm not working on this guy; where's the dude with the bright white briefs?" I worried that if I were in an accident I would have a "little accident" and my clean underwear would be dirty anyway. If I am in an accident, I don't need clean underwear, I need *extra* underwear.

I bet Mom would have been thrilled if just once the evening news reported something like this, "We're going live to the scene of a serious accident at Tenth and Main where they've already requested the police, fire and rescue equipment, and yes, a pair of clean underwear." Later, you would hear, "The police haven't yet released the names of the accident victims but will confirm reports that three of the four were seen wearing bright new underpants. And the fourth? Well, let's just say it's not a pretty sight. His Mom's not going to be happy." Anyway, if you're in an accident today, the hospital isn't looking for clean underwear — they're looking for a Blue Cross card. I was in an accident recently and I didn't get treated until I'd whispered those three little words to the nurse, "I have insurance."

Mom wanted clean underwear. . . just in case. What she really was teaching me was that you never know what can happen. You have to be prepared for the unexpected. Be flexible.

You've got to be flexible these days. You've got to be able to go with the flow. If you don't, you'll be so uptight, you'll spend your entire life miserable. I've had every problem you could have performing on stage and the only way I survived was to adjust. Many of the problems involved animals. I once had a opossum run on stage in the middle of a show. Another time while speaking in a meeting room in a wildlife habitat, a monkey began tapping on the window. But the toughest animal experience was when a bird pooped on my head during a program. It was a direct hit. That's when I understood the true meaning of that old adage, "some days you're a pigeon, some days you're a statue." If I learned one thing through those experiences, it was that you have to be flexible.

We're not very flexible these days. We often seem shocked when tomorrow is not exactly like today. We often hear, "I couldn't believe customers started going elsewhere," or, "I couldn't believe the Dow dipped like that." Or, "It worked for Grandpa, why isn't it working for me?" We need to keep our options open and be flexible. When my oldest daughter, Leah, started talking about college she had her major narrowed down to two choices: Child Psychology or Marine Biology. I'm just glad it wasn't a dual major. I don't think there's a big demand for someone who can psychoanalyze dolphins. She was flexible, she had to be. Trying to take a course that would fit into either major required supreme flexibility. She should have had a major in flexibility. The old Scottish proverb that we've all heard says, "It is better to bend than to break." Everyone needs to be a little more bendable — especially you sock rollers. You know who you are. Your socks are perfectly rolled and placed in precise spots in the drawer according to color and thickness. If the system is disturbed it ruins your whole day. Or you folks who always sit in the same pew in church — Heaven help anyone who sits in your pew. Well, loosen up. You know God can see what's in your heart. He can spot you two rows further back just as easily.

We're all creatures of habit, but some of us creatures are just a little too rigid. I've worked with film directors of commercials and training films who are that way. They think it can only be done one way — their way. One director asked me to deliver my lines with a bit more "lilt." (Wasn't that a hair perm product?) We must have done fifty reads on the script until we got it the one and only way he thought it should be done. He obviously was working by the hour.

When people get set in their ways, animosity is inevitable. Samuel Johnson said, "Life cannot subsist in society but by reciprocal concessions." In other words, virtually every human endeavor is founded on compromise, or being flexible. It certainly is the key to getting along with the opposite sex. We have to accept the differences between the sexes. And we all know there are differences. Take directions, for example. Men don't ask for directions, they're happy as long as they are making good time, but women know every nuance and landmark of the trip. Men don't shop like women, they get a catalog, go into the bathroom and pick out something. Women love scented soap like raspberry shampoo, strawberry creme rinse and banana coconut bath oil soap. It's like taking a shower at International House of Pancakes. Men are the goobers who buy Lava, which is a bar of soap wrapped in 24-grit sandpaper. Because men believe abrasion is how you get clean. Men believe dirty laundry can be resurrected from the dead by tossing it in the dryer and fluffing it up for a while. And men also will never throw clothes away, particularly underwear. There can be nothing left but an elastic band and a man will still hang onto them. They become a family heirloom.

I could go on and on, but the point is that being flexible is the only way to get along with the opposite sex. So be prepared and be flexible by always wearing clean underwear, unless all that's left is an elastic band.

Chapter 9

There's Got To Be Something In There To Eat

Frugality

One thing all kids, from Maine to Hawaii, have in common is their fickleness for food. There's always something they just don't like. The child doesn't exist who likes all food. I'll bet even Andre The Giant, as a kid, despised some food. Most of the time children haven't tried the food they hate. They don't like it simply because it looks nasty, is the wrong color, consistency, or is an adult food.

"How can you not like it when you've never tried it?" Mom used this line when we refused to eat something. Of course, I'd say something like, "Well, I've never gone swimming in a piranha pond and I know I wouldn't like that either." Anyway, if vegetables were so good for you, why did Mom always try to hide them — like putting carrots in orange Jell-O or turnips in my tacos? Why weren't vegetables good enough to sit naked on your plate, just like the cheeseburgers and the chili dogs?

This issue would most often arise when one of us kids got hungry. Invariably we would stare at the refrigerator shelves until the light would nearly burn out and we'd tell Mom, "There's nothing in here." This would prompt Mom's response, "Oh, there's got to be something in there to eat." Well sure, if I'm willing to eat anything. Okay, to Mom's credit, she did have the "10-day Tupperware" rule. We'd throw out whatever was in the Tupperware after ten days, or when we couldn't figure out what it was — whichever came first. Figuring out what was in that Tupperware way in the back of the refrigerator led to some interesting conversations: "Mom, this is either spaghetti or Dad's keeping his bait cold again." Or, "Mom, is cottage cheese ever supposed to be blue?" Or, "I'm not sure, but this stuff is either last week's beef stew or last month's science project."

Well sure, Mom could find something — she is a Mom. She is a good cook. She grew up during the Depression. Now for all of you younger readers, the Depression was when hard times hit the entire country. When I say hard times I don't mean not being able to find the remote control, I mean not being able to find money to pay the mortgage. The Depression was a time when you sometimes (now here comes a phrase many people have never heard) "did without." Mom knew what this was like. That's why she could make something from nothing. She did this a lot. This is how she made her world-famous vegetable soup. We'll never know what was in that soup. Mom kept it a secret. When she went into the kitchen to make this mystery concoction, she banished us from the area, and didn't come out until it was cooking on the stove. A huge pot of "stuff" where every batch was different. It all depended on what was in the refrigerator. It might be vegetables, chicken, beef, eggs, candy, nuts, pretzels, hog jowls, possum bellies, turtle eyes, frog legs, or fishing bait. Whatever happened to be in the refrigerator at the time. All I know is this . . . it was awesome! I don't want to know what was in it because it doesn't matter. It was awesome! Mom's vegetable soup proved two points: first, she's the best cook ever; second, there's always something in the refrigerator to eat.

Mom probably learned that skill out of necessity because she grew up poor. We were also poor as kids but didn't really know it. We did suspect it from time to time, though. Like when Mom would patch our jeans *and* our balloons. On one birthday party she tried to put eight candles on a Twinkie. Mom was trying to teach us to make do with what we have instead of always thinking we need something else. She was dispelling that "grass is greener" theory and she was teaching us frugality.

Frugality is one of those traits nearly everyone used to possess but almost no one has now. That's probably a sign most of us don't remember the Depression and food lines. Or, it's a consequence of easy credit. A lot of people now confuse their MasterCard bill with their mortgage balance, and they have to replace their credit cards twice a year because the numbers wear off.

Whether it's the credit thing or something else, we're just not nearly as frugal as we used to be or should be. We waste and we spend like never before. Most of us do this because we think frugality is only for the poor. Well, let me remind you that most millionaires in the country are frugal because most of them made their money on their own by saving and by taking on debt sparingly. Remember that a poor man will walk a mile to save a buck, but a rich man will walk five.

A lot of people think I'm a little too frugal. My hearing is going bad and I plan on just putting a button in my ear so people will think it's a hearing aid and talk louder. I'll always save a dollar where I can. The only time this concerns me is when I book air travel on those cut-rate airlines. I wonder how they can fly me to Dallas for $19.00. Are they skipping an oil change? The other day they wouldn't let me on a flight because I didn't have correct change. Generally, though, if I can save a dollar, I will. I remember that quote, "If you want to be poor, act rich, and if you want to be rich, act poor." Or, as they tell first-year law students who can borrow just about as much as they want for tuition and living expenses, "If you live like a student now, you'll live like a lawyer later. But if you live like a lawyer now, you'll live like a student later." That's a good rule of thumb.

How financially frugal are you? Have you switched from shining your shoes to painting them? Do you buy your suits from the "left more than thirty days" rack at the dry cleaners? Instead of buying lawn fertilizer have you invested in four cows to which you feed day-old bran muffins? Before going to the beach do you skip the expensive sun blocker and cover yourself with weather-beater semi-gloss? You don't have to go this far, but I bet you could be more frugal. You need to see frugality as a game, and this is a game you really need to win.

So why don't you wait to buy that next necessary purchase from "TURBO-POWERED LAWN TOOLS" until you actually have the money saved and avoid paying hundreds in interest? Consider a used car so you don't have to violate child labor laws and have your kids work to pay for the new one you drove off the showroom floor. In fact, let me help you save your money and give you a comprehensive list of things you just don't need:

1) One of those sport utility vehicles so large that one of the options is a porch swing.

2) Any television set whose screen size is measured in yards. Why would anyone want to see Richard Simmons bigger than he really is (This argument doesn't count if you substitute Christy Brinkley for Richard Simmons. Please allow me this one male chauvinistic comment.)

3) Anything advertised on TV at 3:30 a.m. that promises to make you a millionaire. Outstanding investment opportunities are not found between a program on the new Ginsu nose-hair trimmer and a documentary on solid waste.

4) Any product that no one you know currently owns. This includes fluorescent flea collars or a combination waffle iron and popcorn popper (use the wrong side and this sucker will throw your waffles thirty feet into the air).

5) Anything from the Franklin Mint. Are your grandchildren really going to want your guaranteed limited edition Dukes of Hazard ice cream scoop?

Now I'm not saying you get extreme, enjoy no luxuries, and buy everything in bulk like those 100-pound sacks of cereal from the super centers that take so long to empty the last few morsels are petrified. But I do think you need to stop wasting money on everything from clothing to food. Because there has to be something in there to wear and there has to be something in there to eat.

Chapter 10

Do That One More Time And You're Grounded

Limits

There is always a line — a fine line sometimes — but always a line. As kids, we could foul up, but if we crossed that line, we were grounded. Now there's an interesting term. I assume it was started by some parent who was a pilot, and because it was such a neat metaphor it stuck. What if this term had been started by a jockey? Then you'd be dismounted. Or by a basketball coach, you'd be benched. If a plumber originated it — you'd be flushed.

"Do that one more time and you're grounded," when Mom said it, the game was almost over. It was time to back up and think twice about what you were doing, or at the very least start taking the duct tape off the cat. Pulling pranks is what got me grounded. My brother and I did all the usual stuff — like calling a teacher's house five times and asking for someone who didn't live there (Bill, for example), then calling a sixth time and saying, "Hi, I'm Bill, has anyone called for me?" Or draping a house and trees in toilet paper was a classic. Vaseline on car door latches was a winner, too. But defacing or destroying property was crossing the line, and we knew not to cross it. Spray painting the goldfish was putting yourself into the twilight zone. Same with needling or ribbing someone or joking with them. That was okay too, until it turned caustic or became belittling. There's a name for people who are always caustic or belittling — that name is Don Rickles. Now I know Don is really a nice guy, but as a kid, did he practice by saying, "Sure, I'd like to give you a kiss Aunt Helen, but first I'd like to give you a shave." Or, "Gosh Uncle Ed, is that a new shirt, or did you sew a pocket on the Hungarian flag?" As kids, if we ever got to that point, we had crossed the line.

Mom gave us plenty of rein, but always reminded us that there was a limit. For example, horseplay in the living room was generally okay, but playing with a horse in the living room was crossing the line. Throwing the ball *to* your brother was okay, but throwing a ball *off* of your brother was crossing the line. You get the picture. Anything can be taken too far, and we need to know where that line is. We see this in life all the time. Some comedians tell one joke too many. They should've stopped when they were ahead. Cable TV companies should have stopped at 100 channels in my estimation. We don't need the welding channel or the quilting channel — there is a line! I don't need 200 speed-dial numbers on my cell phone, either. If I can remember that you are number 122, I can probably remember your phone number. And what about 6,882 colors of interior paint, including 137 shades of good ole white. Who decides #136 is "Vanilla Variations" and #137 is "Afternoon In Fresno"? Do we need seven different sizes of Shredded Wheat? It all tastes the same. Do we need 100 flavors of ice cream? Has anyone ever bought Rhubarb-Rutabaga Swirl?

Remember the old story about the elderly man who was in awful health and went to his doctor for a check up? The doctor gave him some advice and prescriptions and sent him on his way. That night the doctor was in a nightclub when he noticed that same elderly patient drinking and dancing with a beautiful young woman. The doctor confronted the old man and asked him what in the world he was doing. The man said he was following the doctor's advice to "be cheerful and get a hot mama." The doctor said, "No, I said be careful you've got a heart murmur." The moral to that story is that exceeding reasonable limits can be detrimental to your health.

There's a limit to what we need and a limit to what we should do. While I'm all for pushing the limit — even to the point of peering over the edge — I'm equally adamant about *not* crossing that line. Why? Because there's no going back. Once you've fallen off the cliff you can't just back up. That's where good judgment comes in, and the average person's judgment is so bad, he runs a risk every time he uses it. You can judge better where that line is if you'll apply a simple rule from Dagobert Runes: "Hesitancy in judgment is the only true mark of a thinker." In other words, wait a minute, and think about whether you're crossing the line. Sometimes we move down the tracks so fast we don't see the line, we just cross it and keep on going.

I was on a plane once when a woman felt her overhead bin space had been robbed from her. While I thought it was entirely appropriate for her to deliver a somewhat stern lecture to the "bin hog" who took it, I looked on in disbelief as she removed his laptop briefcase and intentionally dropped it on the floor from the overhead bin height. She crossed the line.

There are lots of people, in my estimation, who have gone too far. Elizabeth Taylor — what else can you say about a woman who has been to the altar more often than the Pope. What about trash talk television? What a freak fest. Electronic peep shows, often capped by "a final thought" in an earnest, I-feel-your-pain voice that almost comes off as sincere. All in the interest of high ratings. And for that matter, anybody who appears on these shows has crossed the line. All of you — get back to the wacko ward!

Here are some other examples of crossing the line:

Taking not just the mints on the hotel pillow, but the pillow as well.

Sending your tax payment to the IRS in pennies.

Asking your wife to shave your back.

Going to the dentist after you've eaten a pound of garlic.

Putting apple juice in a urine specimen jar and drinking it in front of the nurse.

Having a friend named Jack pick you up at the airport so you can yell, "Hi, Jack!"

Winning the "Truth or Dare" game by eating a box of Tide.

Telling your significant other that the new outfit she bought doesn't make her look fat, it's her big rear end that makes her look fat!

If you've done any of these, you've crossed the line — do it again and you're grounded, or benched, or maybe even flushed.

Chapter 11

Look At The Whole Picture

. . . .

Perspective

. . . .

Even though kids are more resilient than adults, when a child initially meets with disappointment it appears to be the end of the world. An argument with a classmate equates to "*Nobody* likes me." A bad score on one test means "I'm stupid at *everything*!" Missing a movie is met with "I'll *never* get to see it now."

When you're a kid, everything can be a big deal, but usually just to you. Like the day Petey, your hamster, died. Why wasn't that covered on the evening news, huh? Okay, they probably want to know why Petey was found damp and suspiciously close to the Water Pik, but hey, you really loved the little critter. Or how about the time your brother ate seven hot dogs, five pieces of pumpkin pie, and three green apples at the Boy Scout picnic. The evening news could have gotten some great footage if they'd arrived before the ambulance did. After all, how many viewers have actually seen a stomach pumped?

As kids we would blow things completely out of proportion, and those end-of-the-world projections would quickly get Mom to say, "Now let's look at the whole picture." Immediately it wasn't a near-death experience any longer. Mom was always calm and focused on looking at the big picture. I'll bet if she'd been at the siege of the Alamo she'd have said, "What a chance to work on my Spanish; let those guys in." Or, if she'd been on the Titanic, "Look at it this way, we don't have to stop to pick up ice."

Keeping things in perspective is one of the best coping skills you have. And you do that by looking at the big picture. If you have trouble doing that just ask yourself the question, "What is most important?" I bet it's not the size of your house or the horsepower of your car. I bet it's something intangible. I know it's tough to keep the chin up when you come home and your spouse is sitting in front of the television watching the Home Shopping Channel with a bottle of wine and the credit card. It's scary when your daughter says her new 32-year-old boyfriend is still living with his mother until he finds the *right job* that truly challenges him. But remember that everything is good news or bad news — it's just your perspective. The good news is that cigarettes contain 50 percent less tar; the bad news is so do roads. The good news is you like exercise; the bad news is that you get winded playing chess. The good news is your daughter made her first batch of chocolate chip cookies; the bad news is that one of the chips moves. This is just the old "glass is half empty — glass is half full" debate.

James Branch Cabell said, "The optimist proclaims that we live in the best of all possible worlds and the pessimist fears this is true." What is your perspective? Are you a pessimist who feels bad when you feel good for fear that you'll feel worse when you feel better? Are you the one who complains about the noise when opportunity knocks? How do you look at life? I'm not saying you should be a Pollyanna and always look at life through those rose-colored glasses, but they should be a little lighter than the specs worn by Ray Charles. Just lighten up a little. Ask yourself what was worrying you a year ago or six months ago or a month ago. I'll bet you can't remember and I'll bet that six months from now you won't be able to remember what's troubling you today. Do you see the big picture?

A long time ago I heard a motivational speaker who had lost both legs to a land mine during World War II. He said when he filled out job applications under the heading "height" he would put "adjustable." Remember that old college prank where a student writes a letter to his parents telling them about his recent car crash, drug conviction, and girlfriend's prison sentence. He then wrote, "P.S. — All of the above is false, but I did fail a chemistry test and I wanted you to keep it in perspective."

Sometimes we can't see the whole picture because the problem is too close to us. We need to create some distance. That's what the most important question can do. It allows us to see the big picture. If you're a parent, one of your first most important moments is the first time you hold your child in your arms. You're not thinking about how much it will cost you to send him or her to college, or about all the late nights you'll be up waiting for your child to come home. You should be thinking about those things, but you don't. Why? Because there are times, and this is one of them, when Mother Nature has a way of making you focus on the here and now, and all the rest will work itself out.

There are lots of other important moments for a parent. Like sending the kids off to the first day of school, and sending off the last college tuition check. Or watching their first steps in football cleats, or high heels, or golf shoes (and if you've got a child who's worn all three, they're either very talented or very troubled). Or the day they bring home their first paycheck which you hope is before the day you get your first Social Security check. Or the day they move out . . . hopefully, it's before the day they get *their* first Social Security check.

Dr. C.W. Metcalf offers another way of keeping things in perspective: He tells people to keep a "joy list." This is a list of the little things in life that are guaranteed to make you smile. Keep that list with you and refer to it during those tough times. My list includes a time when my daughter, Lindsay, and I decided to speak in a British accent all day. We went from mall to grocery store to fast food joint, and spoke in this bogus foreign accent just to see what the people around us would do. The more attention we garnered, the heavier the accent got. It was a scream. We still laugh about it to this day and it's one of those memories of my daughter that I'll take to my grave.

Or when my eldest daughter, Leah, insisted on going with me on a trip. She had been driving for about three years and said she could help me drive. She slept the entire trip to the engagement and the entire trip back. Now whenever she asks to go on a trip, she says she'll "help drive." We immediately burst into laughter.

I know it's tough to keep things in perspective when you get a letter saying you are *not* a finalist for the Publisher's Clearing House Sweepstakes *or* you've drug your luggage at midnight all the way to the end of the hall only to find out your hotel room key doesn't work *or* the tattoo artist shrieks, "Eagle! I thought you said beagle!" When these things happen, remember to step back, glance at your "joy list," ask what's most important . . . and look at the big picture.

Chapter 12

That Will Stunt Your Growth

Thinking Long Term

My mother was not a trained nutritionist, but she always preached the value of a good, balanced diet. She encouraged us to eat plenty of vegetables. That's why every day I have Corn Nuts. My mom was a great cook. We ate healthy, and we ate a lot. We didn't skip meals, and there were certain foods and drinks that would stunt your growth, so they were taboo.

I remember at about the age of 12 trying to take a sip of my Dad's coffee. "Put that down," she scolded, "it'll stunt your growth." I immediately picked up the coffee can and said, "Look at these Hills Brothers. They look full size to me."

I really didn't think the wrong food would stunt your growth. I thought it was some of those other things that would stunt your growth. Like, playing peewee football against ten year olds who had five o'clock shadows. Like selling photocopies of your sister's diary. Like taking your first ride on the 10-speed bike, downhill. Those were the things I thought would stunt your growth. But I didn't want to completely doubt my Mom, and I didn't want to be a runt, so I ate a lot of the good things. And it showed.

When I was entering my Sophomore year in high school, I was four feet, eleven inches tall and I weighed 96 pounds. I was a massive specimen of a man. How did my growth get stunted? I did all the right things, I ate all the right foods. Conversely, my baby brother in high school reached six feet and 200 pounds on a steady diet of Cheetos and Ding Dongs. My brother believed a balanced diet was Ho Hos on one side of the plate and Twinkies on the other. But as was nearly always the case, Mom was right. My growth wasn't stunted, it just came late.

Mom wanted me to take the long-term view. She didn't want me to do something I would regret later in life, and even though she knew coffee wouldn't keep me from reaching six feet tall, she nonetheless made me think about today's actions affecting tomorrow.

I wish more people would think more long term. We are ridiculously impulsive. We need to think more about the future, because as that old saying goes, "that's where I'm going to spend the rest of my life."

Some pundits say we are a more stupid society than yesteryear's. I disagree. We are a more impulsive society. That characteristic can give the impression of being a little short on cerebral activity. All the get-rich-quick schemes are a great example of how impulsive we are. My Grandpa used to say, the only way to double your money is to fold it in half.

Home pregnancy tests are an example of how impulsive we are. I know it can be very exciting to find out if you're pregnant, but isn't this when we should take the time to consult a medical professional? You don't see home tonsillectomy kits, and nobody has ever marketed do-it-yourself brain surgery.

The guy who races by, "I can't talk right now. I'm really late for my course on how to relax." Or the man who says, "I've read the book, now I want to listen to the tape, watch the video *and* use the daily planner, so I can simplify my life," are examples of people who are slightly impulsive.

There's a word for people who don't think long term, who are concerned only about doing what will benefit them today. I think that word is "Congress." And, for that matter, anybody who drinks vodka isn't thinking long term. Vodka doesn't leave an odor on your breath, you'd much rather have people know you're drunk, than think you're stupid. Think it through. Quit being so impulsive.

Our being impulsive is why we see all those ludicrous warning labels on products. The "not to be taken orally" warning on the Vaseline jar is because some impulsive nitwit thought, "I wonder what this tastes like," without pausing and reflecting on the long-term consequences of his actions. Same with the "Do not drive with auto visor in place," warning on the back of that car sun shield. Yep, somebody tried driving with it in place. They were in a hurry.

When I see "apply directly to eyes" directions on the bottle of eye drops, I have to ask, has anyone ever said, "I've got a terrible toothache, do we have any Murine?" Or the warning label on the gas-powered leaf blower that says, "not for use indoors." Folks, if you've got leaves in your living room, I submit you have a roofing problem.

Impulsive people do silly things. I know they give comedy writers great material, but I'd rather see them think long term. Think down the road. Ask, "What does this mean next week or next year," instead of impulsively acting out every whim that comes to mind.

The popularity of psychic hot lines is a perfect example of how impulsive we are. Think about it. If they were really psychic, they would be calling you, because they would know you wanted to talk to them. If they were psychics they would have bought Pfizer stock before the release of Viagra and now be sunbathing in Bermuda. I guarantee you they wouldn't be listening to someone who saw a 1-900 number on TV and called for career counseling and direction in their love life. Why don't you test these so-called psychics. The next time you lose your car keys. . . call them. The next time you can't find your car in the parking lot. . .ring them up on your cell phone. See how psychic they are then.

If you still believe in psychics and want to use them, here's how you can tell the person you're talking to is *not* a psychic: They answer your call with "hello," and they ask for a credit card number. Folks, if they knew where to find you a good job, would they be working where they have to answer the phone at one o'clock in the morning?

Thinking long term allows us to look at the big picture and make more intelligent decisions. You're not thinking long term, when at the age of 16, you tattoo the name of your girlfriend or boyfriend on your arm, or some embarrassing place. You're not thinking long term, if you race through that yellow light. Unless, of course, you want to be *away* for the long term. In contrast you are thinking long term if you plant tulip bulbs or if you make seven year olds take piano lessons.

It was James Allen who said, "You are today, where your thoughts have brought you. You will be tomorrow, where your thoughts take you."

We need to just think a little bit more. Even a goat does his best work with his head. Thinking long term just makes life easier. Hard work is often the easy work you didn't do at the right time, probably because you were too impulsive. By not thinking long term, we have a tendency then, to make the same mistakes over and over again. Remember, man is the only animal who can be skinned more than once. And nothing causes us to lose our hides more quickly than impulsive thinking.

The options are obvious. Be impulsive or think long term. It's easier to be impulsive because we see the results immediately. We get immediate feedback. But . . . it'll stunt your growth.

Chapter 13

Chew Your Food With Your Mouth Shut

· ·

Annoyance

· ·

S mackers. That's what Mom called people who chewed their food with their mouths slightly open, sounding like two pieces of liver smacking together.

Mom could hear a smacker from a hundred feet away. That wasn't the only sound she could detect at long distances. She could hear things like a cookie jar lid opening. If I had gone for the cookies while Mom was away, it would not have surprised me to hear the phone ring and Mom at the other end saying: "Mark, I'm over at your Grandmother's and you know you're not to eat cookies this close to dinner, so put that lid back on." Mom could hear anything, like that little click when I opened the front door after missing my curfew. But when Mom heard a smacker, you could count on hearing one of Mom's most rigid rules: "Chew your food with your mouth shut!" That smacking didn't bother Mom because it demonstrated a lack of the social graces. Nor was she worried that the smacking would lead to drooling half-eaten food onto your clean clothes. It just plain annoyed her. Mom wanted us to realize that it's okay to care enough about other people to not annoy them.

Now I'm not talking about physical annoyances. Like when the windshield wiper streaks and the streak is exactly in your line of sight. Or when the toilet clogs up right before company comes over. Or when you pull that little piece of skin by a hangnail that then tears all the way to your elbow. Physical annoyances aren't the worse kind. I'm talking about people annoying people.

Some of us have taken this to new heights. You know who I'm talking about . . . those people who talk loudly enough on the plane or any public place, so everyone can listen to their dazzling conversations. I've mentioned this before, but it's one of my biggest pet peeves. These people are certain we're as interested in hearing their voices as they are. Yadda, Yadda, Yadda. And they love to whip out their cell phones and talk loud so we can hear them close that "shower curtain ring" deal. Has anyone ever told these loud people they are annoying? Hopefully they are reading this right now. Even so, it won't matter — they're not that considerate. These are the people who leave the last sip of milk in the milk container instead of buying a new gallon. Or they leave that last square of toilet tissue on the roll instead of replacing it. Then you're relegated to using a paper towel or an old used napkin from Taco Bell that has hot taco sauce on it, which gives new meaning to the term "run for the border."

The used car television commercials with that guy yelling at the camera are annoying. If I want it that loud, I'll turn up the volume. You may remember the dealership's name, but only because you were annoyed, that's not a good thing. If that dealership guy really wants me to listen to his sales pitch, here's a suggestion: Hire the announcer who whispers throughout the golf tournaments. You have to listen real close to hear what he's saying. If he can make viewers pay attention to a three-foot putt, he can make them concentrate on the splendors of a four-door Buick.

And what about telemarketing people? If I want my carpet cleaned, or if I want to switch long distance phone service, I'll do it myself. Quit bugging me at dinnertime. Here's how I suggest we get rid of those pests: Forget Caller ID. How about Caller TNT? Once you know it's a telemarketer, hit a button and BOOM! They won't bother anybody anymore.

Still there is nothing as annoying as daytime network TV. It's either giggling local news anchors (I get the feeling they've spent more on their dental work than on their education), sharing an exclusive report on the history of the corn dog, or it's trash television. People at the lower end of the food chain attempting to discuss publicly the nuances of why their overweight, transvestite, strip-dancing lover ran off with their mother-in-law. My question for any of those trash talk hosts, or electronic ringmasters as I prefer to call them is, "I can see where you might find one cross-dressing, Canadian carpenter, but where the heck do you find three that will appear together?" The scariest thing about these shows is: Who are the folks we don't see? Trash TV isn't new, of course. Lots of us still remember "The Newlywed Game," and the rude and crude questions those folks would answer in search of prizes. As George Carlin once said about that show: "The things people will tell about each other just for a set of matched luggage."

Where do these people come from? They weren't born pests, were they? Is there a school that teaches people to be annoying? A classroom of would-be Eddie Haskells where everybody takes turns scraping their fingernails on the black-board. They must have had some help along the way: parents who ignored them, or classmates who made fun of them. Let me just say that if there is such a school, don't visit the cafeteria! Enough said.

Horace Mann said, "Manners easily and rapidly mature into morals." So stop annoying me. Wait your turn in line. Don't tailgate me on the interstate. Quit bumping into me as you rush off the plane so you then can *wait* for your luggage. Sit down in front of me at the concert. Don't call me on the phone during the ball game. Blow your cigarette smoke in some direction other than my face. Don't talk to me nose to nose. Stop taking all the covers. Don't ask me questions when Sports Center is on. Quit seeking my opinion about your clothes when you already have formed an opinion, but most of all: Chew your food with your mouth shut.

Chapter 14

Stop Looking At Your Brother

••••••••••••••••••••••••

Conflict Resolution

••••••••••••••••••••••••

Nothing irritates a sibling like staring. It's perfect antagonism, because technically you can argue that you're not doing anything. You're not hurting them, saying anything to them, or messing with their stuff. It's not like that trick where Mom says, "Stop touching your brother." Then you place your index finger a millimeter away from his earlobe and chant, "I'm not touching you! I'm not touching you!"

But just looking is not really doing anything and can be the most irritating harassment of all. My brother's forehead was like a human bull's eye. He might as well have had a tattoo on his forehead that said, "Stare at this spot." I never stopped staring at my brother because it never stopped bothering him. We had our roles down better than the actors in the one thousandth performance of "Our Town."

Brother: Stop it!

Me: I'm not doing anything!

Brother: You are too!

Me: I am not!

Brother: Are too!

Me: Am not!

Mom: What's going on in there?

Brother: He's bothering me!

Me: I'm not doing anything!

Brother: He is too!

Mom: Leave your brother alone!

Me: I'm not touching him!

This can go on forever without a winner. It's just like playing tic-tac-toe. It's a pointless activity. It's like the dog chasing its tail or me chasing Eva Longoria.

Staring is a pointless activity with no winner, that can go on and on if you're good at it. I have staring down to an art form. I learned there is a fine line between staring and leering, but there is a difference. I think my attorney will back me up on this one. Staring is what a guy does to upset his brother. Leering is what he does to a female. And beyond leering there is, of course, drooling; but since this is a family-oriented book, I won't go into that.

Staring is always a neat way to bug your brother because it activates that sense of insecurity we all feel during adolescence. (If you're still bugging your brother by staring and you're over thirty, might I suggest you seek professional help.) Anyway, it's that period of time in your life when you definitely don't want to call attention to yourself in any way, and somebody staring at you can make you go bonkers. You wonder if your ears are on straight, or if they're too big, or if you're wearing a "cool" shirt. Those are the kinds of embarrassing questions going through your mind when you're being stared at. And that's why I did it. I did it to bug my brother. The whole point of this was simple harassment. I had no purpose other than to get a reaction from my brother. I just wanted to see him squirm, get upset, bothered, frustrated, and mad. I was his brother, this was my job. Had he not reacted I would have stopped. It wouldn't have been fun anymore.

I now realize making people mad on a full-time basis could have qualified me for many adult jobs. Like working any job in any office of the Department of Motor Vehicles. Or working as a convenience store clerk who tries to sell you something, anything, in addition to what you're buying. "Sir, wouldn't you like a prune smoothie to go with that jar of mustard?" So it was my job to get my brother to react; and he always did. He was my brother, that was his job. Then Mom would get in the foray and cease the event with that compelling mandate: "Stop looking at your brother." The whole point of this edict was to stop the conflict. Mom wasn't acting as a mediator, a moderator, or negotiator, she was a dictator. She wasn't interested in hearing what inner turmoil I was feeling (the only inner turmoil I ever felt was caused by eating an entire box of red hots in 8.2 seconds). Mom never "felt my pain." Mom planned on causing my pain if I didn't stop bugging my brother. She knew that both of us were acting about as rationally as mice in a cheese factory. And she knew that she had to jump in between us brothers because we wouldn't stop it ourselves. We couldn't remember who started it, but neither one of us was going to stop it. Just like the Hatfields and McCoys or high-profile ethnic wars throughout the world, parties have been fighting with each other so long, many of them don't even know why they're fighting anymore. Too many conflicts around the world are too similar to those "did-not/did-too" kind of futile dialogs.

We've had many of these situations over time. What was the deal with that one-hundred-year war we all studied in history class? What the heck was that about? Is this something to be proud of? To say your relatives were in a war so long that it started with rocks and ended with rifles. I always heard that a long dispute meant both parties were wrong. Now, don't misunderstand me. I'm not suggesting that we can't disagree. It's healthy to disagree. Because when two people agree on everything, one of them is unnecessary. But when we establish an argument only by noise and command, it shows that our reason is weak. We must use more than noise and command, someone must be willing to take that first step at compromise. Conflict resolution often doesn't occur because neither party will stand up and say, "I'm stopping this." Neither party will blink. Neither party will take the *first* step to stop it. Well, it's time to stop it, because in the big picture, we are all brothers, so stop touching your brother. Stop looking at him. Just stop it.

Chapter 15

Put That Down Before You Break It

· ·

Accountability

· ·

A store I remember going into when I was a kid had the following sign: "Lovely to look at, nice to hold; if you break it, we mark it sold." That was probably the reasoning behind Mom's "Put-It-Down" rule. Like all mothers, she understood that kids just can't look at something while it's sitting there. They have to pick it up to look at it, and the odds of them dropping it are similar to the odds that your cat will hurl a hairball right after you clean the carpet, almost guaranteed. Mom knew we would drop it, probably break it, and she would then have to pay for it. Then we'd go and try to break something else. Kids can break anything. Moms know this. The other day at Firestone I heard, "Tommy, put down that snow tire." Now if you don't have kids, that may sound strange, but parents know that a tire, which can cruise over 14 railroad spikes and still go 60,000 miles, is in danger in Tommy's hands.

Mom was very emphatic about her "Put-It-Down" rule. She would often give us the double warning: "I don't want you to touch anything. I don't want you to even think about touching anything." This rule about putting things down wasn't so much about keeping your hands off things as much as it was about accountability. Mom wanted us to be accountable for our actions. Mom was tired of our actions affecting her wallet, and she clearly let us know that if "You break it, you buy it."

What a novel concept . . . accountability. People being held accountable for their actions and words. It's no wonder many youths don't get that concept anymore. We tell our kids they can't get ahead unless they "hit the books." Then they see a star athlete with a *book* contract after he *hits* his coach. The papers are rife with examples of people not being held accountable for their actions. Large corporate executives making poor decisions forcing the company into layoffs. Do you remember who got laid off? Not the overpaid pampered executive who decided the company's marketing strategy — it was the employee just doing what he was told to do. The order taker was let go and the order maker kept his job. When cars aren't selling who does Detroit lay off? The folks who make them; not the guys who decided Americans wanted a bright orange gas guzzler that cost more than most folks' first home. When corporate profits are down, it's the guy on the shop floor who gets the pink slip, not the executive who's walking on an office floor of Guatemalan walnut that leads to his private bathroom which includes a hot tub the size of the Florida panhandle.

Not enough of us are held accountable anymore. I think we ought to hold the weather forecasters more accountable for their work. They need a penalty if they are wrong. I'll bet that would improve their forecasting. Put some pressure on them. In no other work can you be wrong half of the time and get promoted. What if you went into the office of your boss and said, "There's a 20 percent chance I'm going to get that report to you." He would say, "There is a 100 percent chance you're fired!"

Weather forecasters now are so often wrong they try to distract you by spending more and more time talking about the weather far away or by talking about dumb weather facts. Am I the only one who's noticed this? Two minutes of my TV weather cast is spent on local conditions, and the other six minutes are spent on a low-pressure situation over Lithuania, or the history of sleet.

People are let off the hook too easily. If you don't believe that, compare the list of convicted felons to the list of prison inmates. They are not the same. They were convicted but then had the sentence reduced or were paroled; teaching them that they don't have to be accountable for their actions. Instead of hard time, they're often doing community service. Here's my suggestion for community service — have the criminal move away from the community.

Remember when we used to have that "lock them up and throw away the key" mentality? We can't throw it away anymore, but can we at least hide it for a few more years. That may be too extreme, but I wish we would err a little more often in that direction. We teach that it's all right to do wrong. Look how often we allow athletes to get away with a wide variety of bad behavior and still allow them to play on game day. Some athletes spend less time on the cover of *Sports Illustrated* than they do on *True Detective*. It's getting so bad, I don't know where I'll see the most athletes on television: on ESPN or on "America's Most Wanted." Is it just a coincidence that accountability and responsibility rhyme? These seem to be the things we dread the most, but in my estimation, they are the things that develop manhood and womanhood the most. We dodge cars, we dodge taxes, and we dodge responsibilities. We are always demanding our rights, but never demanding accountability or responsibility.

Does the phrase, "You made your bed, now sleep in it," mean anything anymore? A lot of us don't grasp the concept of accountability because we see everybody getting away with everything. Let's change that. Here's what I propose: A real eye-for-an-eye policy. If the plumber leaves a mess when he fixes your sink, you're allowed to go to his house and dump water on his floor and scratch the woodwork. If the present you ordered for Aunt Myrtle doesn't show up, you're allowed to go to the customer service representative's house who promised the delivery and pick something out for your Aunt. And if the guy at the airport counter announces a five-minute delay and it turns into an hour, you get his watch. Time obviously means nothing to him anyway.

People often avoid accountability by rationalizing. Here's an example. Some studies show hops can reduce the risk of cancer. Hops are used in the brewing of beer, therefore, beer can reduce the risk of cancer. Beer then must be a health food . . . some people can rationalize anything. Some people can always find an excuse or an explanation in an attempt to avoid accountability. They can rationalize their behavior by saying "my Momma spanked me as a kid," or "I got caught up in the emotion of the crowd." These are common cop outs for bad behavior. It's another way of saying "it's not my fault." When I was growing up, the common cop out was "I was trying to find myself." This was an acceptable excuse for many people. It didn't work in my house though. When I was two, I knew who I was, where I was, what I was supposed to do, and what part of my anatomy would get it if I didn't.

We all need to be more accountable for our actions. Put away the old "Daddy-will-take-care-of-it-for-me," thinking. Put away the "I'm-going-to-get-mine-to-heck-with-you," mentality. And put that down before you break it.

Chapter 16

Recite Your ABC's

●●●●●●●●●●●●●●●●●●●●●●●

Fundamentals

●●●●●●●●●●●●●●●●●●●●●●●●

Without Mom's influence I might have been 20 before I learned my ABC's. This is generally the way I operated: After I did something once . . . I was ready to move on to another conquest. This may have been one of the reasons Mom accused me of attention deficit disorder, which, of course, is ridiculous. I've always been able to concentrate on . . . whatever . . . er . . . what was I writing about? Oh, that's right, ABC's. After I recited them the first time I said, "Okay, I've recited them, now what?" Once I had recited my ABC's I was ready to move on and learn something else — anatomy, biology, sex education — the usual stuff that comes after the

ABC's. But Mom knew I hadn't really learned them yet, so she made me recite my ABC's over and over and over. Anywhere, anytime, anyplace.

"Mark, show Aunt Modena you know your ABC's."

"Aw, Mom, it's midnight and I'm eighteen."

Mom never asked us to show other things we learned at school. For instance, I took a shop class, but Mom never said, "Come in here and build your aunt a birdhouse." There's just something about the alphabet. Why did I have to keep repeating it? If I ever forgot how it went, isn't it written down somewhere, like on the top of every blackboard of every grammar school in America, for Pete's sake. But I still had to recite them, even when I tried a smart-aleck answer like, "Okay, I'll recite them, do you want them in alphabetical order?"

I said my ABC's until I could say them in my sleep or sing them. Everyone knows that ABC song. It's the educational equivalent of the theme from "The Beverly Hillbillies." It sticks with you like heartburn after jalapeños. It got to where the only way I could say my ABC's was to sing that stupid song. It sometimes would get stuck in my head and I would be humming or whistling it for hours (you may be doing that right now). To this day, when I look up a word in the dictionary I have to sing the ABC song to myself. Sometimes in public places without knowing it I'm singing out loud, bouncing my head back and forth, inviting others to sing along: "Everybody sing!"

"A-B-C-D-E-F-G-"

"H-I-J-K-L-M-N-O-P-"

"Q-R-S-"

"T-U-V-"

"W-X-"

"Y and Z"

"Now I've said my ABC's, tell me what you think of me."

Mom was probably preparing me for that day in the future when I would be stopped at a sobriety checkpoint and asked to say my ABC's. That's tough duty. They shine that eye-blinding laser light used in tanning beds right in your face, then ask you to perform without the benefit of a dress rehearsal. This is not fair. But Mom prepared me, I just start singing. I'm on stage. I have it choreographed and everything. I've waited for this moment for a long time.

"A-B-C-D-E-F-G . . . come on, put your hands together now!"

"H-I-J-K-L-M-N-O-P . . . everybody sing!"

"Q-R-S . . . here we go!"

"T-U-V . . . feel the music!"

"W-X . . . we're groovin' now!"

"Y and Z . . . Hallelujah!"

"Now I've said my ABC's, tell me what you think of me!"

"I think you must have been dropped on your head as a kid."

Recite your ABC's, say your ABC's, do your ABC's . . . Mom wanted it to become habit. I remember hearing once that habit is a cable, where we weave a thread of it each day and it becomes so strong we cannot break it. Mom wanted our ABC's to become a habit so strong it couldn't be broken. That was important to Mom because the ABC's are the basis of language. If you don't know your ABC's, you can't perform language skills. And Mom knew that every activity had its own set of ABC's *or*, the basics. The ABC's of any activity are the fundamentals. Miss out on the fundamentals and you don't perform the job. It is the foundation; and I've always said, if you don't build a strong foundation, then you probably built my first house. But that's another story.

Mastering the ABC's — the basics — of anything are first and foremost. Take the ABC's of human behavior for example. This is a chance for me to share with you the one piece of educational psychology I learned in college . . . I figure this tidbit of information cost me around $8,000. The ABC's of human behavior stand for **A**ntecedent, **B**ehavior, and **C**onsequence. *Antecedent* is what precedes the desired behavior. It's the command, request, or promise. *Behavior* is the action that occurs, *Consequence* is the outcome of that behavior. For years, many people taught that if you wanted a particular behavior to occur you needed to spend more time on the Antecedent. In other words, make a better command, or promise more, or close the sale. It doesn't take a Freud to figure out the fallacy of this deduction. A good Antecedent will create a desired behavior once, but if you want that behavior to occur over and over again, there must be a consequence that encourages it.

When I was young, my mother would walk in and see me lying on the couch watching "Leave It To Beaver," and deliver the Antecedent, "Mark, go mow the yard." My behavior was to continue lying on the couch. The reason was there was no bad consequence if I didn't go mow the yard. But if my Dad walked in and delivered the very same Antecedent, my behavior was entirely different. I got out there and mowed that yard as fast as I could, because I knew what the consequence was if I didn't.

Businesses often make promises (Antecedents) to get customers in the door in hopes of boosting sales (Behavior). The customers that have a bad experience (Consequence) may never come back. These ABC's are the basics of human behavior. Know them and you will become better at existing with people. The world is full of people that are good with promises (Antecedents), but are bad at delivering those promises (Behaviors). Mom had another way of saying this,

"It's not what you say, it's what you do." Actions do speak louder than words.

You often hear school officials say, "It's time we got back to the basics: Reading, Writing and Arithmetic." But there are lots of schools that don't have to go back because they never forgot the basics. That's why their students are way out front. And in some areas of human endeavor ignoring the fundamentals can be downright dangerous. You don't skydive until you've packed and unpacked your parachute so many times you could do it in your sleep. And any private pilot worth his wings double-checks the maintenance done on his plane. And you'd better believe Superman made sure his tights were run-proof.

Do you know your ABC's of human behavior? Do you know the ABC's of your specific job? Are you fundamentally sound, or have you skipped the basics so you can just get going? It's time we got back to the basics and re-learned our ABC's. So the next time you're having problems with a task, ask yourself if you skipped over those fundamentals. If you take care of the basics, life is much happier. It'll make you break out into a song . . . probably that ABC song.

Chapter 17

You Have Plenty Of Clothes To Wear

Appreciation

In caveman times, clothing selection was easy. You knew what you were going to wear every day. It was what you wore yesterday and slept in last night. Krunk never went whining to his Mom, "I don't have anything to wear for the mastodon hunt today." They probably still complained, though. You can bet cavewomen pulled aside that boulder, looked into that closet and said, "Tell me the truth, does this hippo-hide dress make me look like a hippo?"

Of course, cavemen and cavewomen weren't our only ancestors who didn't worry about their wardrobe — how about the women who settled the Old West? All their dresses were made from flour sacks; how many choices could you have? Did your Great, Great Grandmother ever say, "Hmm . . . should that flour label be in the front or back?" Or how about Adam and Eve . . . Adam never had to choose between boxers and briefs — it was leaves all the way. And Eve? About the only choice she had was after the apple incident when she started wearing a cross-your-heart fern. Shopping for new clothes was pretty easy then. All you needed was a machete.

The story is a little different today. We have too many clothing options and too many social directives. Deciding what to wear becomes difficult. I would tell Mom there was nothing clean, and she would look in my closet and say, "You have plenty of clothes to wear." Well, not in my mind. When you are an adolescent, there is a "cool" standard you must meet. The brand of jeans you wore last week may not be "in" anymore, and you can't be caught dead in them, because they make you look too skinny, or too fat, or too short, or too normal. Clothing is a statement-maker for youth. Always has been; always will be. My parents thought my bell bottoms, bib overalls, and platform shoes were just as stupid as I think today's kids' clothing statements are. My clothes may have been odd, but at least they fit. How do kids buy trousers today? Take their size and then cube it? It looks like they could sublet their Levis. That's the opposite of when I was a kid. I swear I had a pair of jeans I had to get into with a shoehorn. The first time I wore them my Mom said, "Where did those come from, an aerosol can?" You know what kind I mean, if you had change in your front pockets, people could read the dates.

Mom wasn't really nixing our clothing tastes as much as she was saying, "The closet isn't half-empty, it's half-full. Be grateful for what you have. Cicero said, "Gratitude is not only the greatest of all virtues, but the parent of all others." Mom wanted us to appreciate the clothes we had, which were perfectly fine, and to stop thinking we had to make heads turn with every outfit. More than once she reminded us that a lot of other kids had no clothing options. And she would remind us that earlier in our lives we had few clothing options ourselves. We stopped appreciating them over time as our standard of living went up. We stopped appreciating the little things, and then we stopped appreciating the big things. The radio became a black-and-white television that gave way to a color television which begat the really big screen television that evolved to a high-def flat screen and then to 3-D and before you know it, we get miffed because the "picture-in-a-picture" option isn't working. We're not happy until we own absolutely everything in that Brookstone catalog. We're convinced we've got to have that vibrating massage bed and the Elvis Presley jukebox. The amazing thing about these catalogs is that they convince us that we absolutely must have stuff we didn't even know *existed*. "Wow, a combination potato peeler and flashlight! Why, they're right, what if there is a power failure while I'm fixing dinner." Sometimes I want to tell people to take a few steps back in time. Then see if you can appreciate what you've got. We're all guilty of wanting more. In fact, I can see this happening in the not-too-distant future:

> The union vs. management battle had been long and hard, and the strike had taken a toll on both sides, but finally the union leader stood in front of his fellow members. "Ladies and gentlemen," he said, "We've finally got the wages and the working conditions we want, but I'm here to announce that under the new contract you'll only have to work on Mondays." The wild cheering had just begun as a fellow in the back asked, "*Every* Monday?"

I'm as guilty as anybody else in forgetting how easy we have it. I complain about being forced to buy 2 percent milk when the store is out of skim. But it wasn't that long ago when, as a kid on the farm, I milked a cow every morning and night just to obtain our milk. Oh that was a chore I relished. I did that every day through my teens until I got a little older and a little wiser. . . and a little brother. Then *he* milked that cow every day. Through that, though, I learned that cows don't give milk, you have to take it from them — sometimes fight them for it. And when I think about it, I really can't complain about the 2 percent milk. I just appreciate it's fresh and in a container; and I'm not fighting over any bovine rights to it. The only problem I face now is when I read the imprint that says, "Must sell by October 10." Well, I went door-to-door trying to sell it to my neighbors but they already had their own. Now I'm worried, what if I don't sell it by then.

I, like any other parent, have tried to give my kids everything I didn't have. This is exactly why our standard of living goes up from generation to generation. I tried to make sure they ate well and wore good clothes and drove nice cars, unlike the cars I drove as a kid. For years I drove clunkers. Cars that had so little power they would slow down when you turned on the radio. You always made sure they had jumper cables and a tow rope in the trunk because they broke down every other trip. I remember trading in one when the car dealer asked me to pull it on a truck scale so he could weigh it. You know you have a bad car when someone buys it by the pound.

I want a better life for my kids. That sometimes makes it difficult to teach appreciation, because to appreciate something you often have to go without it. You see the "Catch-22" here? I don't want them to go without. If you don't believe that, look at my two daughters' shoe and clothing collections.

They made money last summer by conducting bus tours of their closets. All I can do is remind them that they do have the important things in life and that they need to appreciate what they do have. And that they really do have plenty of clothes to wear.

Chapter 18

You Can Have That When You Prove To Me You're Going To Be Good

· ·

Behavior

· ·

Y ou had to be good to get "stuff" in our house. Stuff was
scarce, but what there was required good behavior. And
there was no stuff on the installment plan. It cost you cash.
Cash meant quality behavior. Mom made us earn the good
stuff by saying, "You can have that when you prove to me

you're going to be good." Don't just tell me you're going to be good — prove it.

Of course, as a kid being good is relative. If you were better than your nearest relative, say your brother, you could expect some stuff. That meant you could do bad things as long as it wasn't as bad as what your brother did. Which meant there were often conversations like this in our house: "Okay, Mom, you're right. I did put the cat in the dryer, but so did Jay, and he didn't use the delicate cycle."

Mom's idea of getting the goodies after you've been good ought to be applied everywhere. What if we told Congress, "I'll send in my taxes when you prove you're spending my previous payments responsibly." What if sports team owners said, "Listen, Bruiser, you'll get that forty-bezillion-dollar contract when you spend as much time on the practice field as you do at the police station." It's a simple concept — you get it when you're good. That principle is reinforced by one of the nuggets of information I learned in college. Here's the nugget: Behavior doesn't lie. People can tell you anything, but the best indicator of their current behavior is their past behavior.

When I went through a tax audit a few years ago, the examiner told me over the phone what I needed to bring and told me not to worry because she was very reasonable and easy to work with. Ironically, a friend of a friend had experienced an audit with the same examiner a few years before. I couldn't believe this person could remember the name of the examiner. He said, "After the audit, you won't forget her name either." When the audit began, I tried to diffuse the tension by offering a couple of stock comedic lines about tax audits. She asked to see my records, and I retorted, "My Neil Diamond collection or the Doobie Brothers?" She said, "Some of these deductions look funny." I said, "So laugh, they're supposed to be funny; I'm a comedian." I asked if she would allow my $10,000-a-year contribution to the family of the Unknown

Soldier. Apparently she had heard those old lines before. She was stone-faced. This auditor had the personality of an undertaker with the gout. I wasn't expecting loud guffaws, a small grin would have been nice. It was then I realized not all examiners are zany, off-the-wall, madcaps. It was also then I realized the person over the phone who had assured me she would be a no-problem, walk-in-the-park examiner, had been lying. She said she was very reasonable and easy to work with. Right! She was about as easy to work with as a kite in a hurricane! Just like the friend of a friend had told me — her past behavior didn't lie. I wonder what this examiner was like growing up. Was she the kind of kid who said, "Mom, you gave him 37 M&M's and I only got 36."

I took a course on interviewing and the most important point I gleaned from the instruction was to identify behaviors, not attitudes. Anyone can lie about attitudes. It's much tougher to lie about a specific behavior. For example, don't ask a question like, "Do you like to read?" Instead, ask, "Tell me about the last two books that you read." Behavior doesn't lie. This premise is why I seldom (roughly twice a year) fall for the 'get rich schemes' on late night TV infomercials. They're telling you how to make a million bucks. Well the secret is, you're watching how they did it — can you say "fleece"? If someone can make a million bucks, wouldn't they be doing it instead of trying to hawk mundane CDs filled with motivational platitudes? You can't make a million bucks with advertising working from your home. You can't buy houses with no money down. And you can't have anything you want if you follow the four secret steps to success — I know this because I did the four steps and Heather Locklear never showed up.

Okay, there are some exceptions to my rantings. There are houses you can buy with no money down, if you can get the dog to move out. The no-money-down houses are the ones the real estate agents call fixer-uppers. When you see or hear that term, look out. They spent less time rebuilding Berlin. No-money-down houses usually don't come with wall-to-wall carpeting. They also don't come with wall-to-wall floors.

While we're talking about late-night television infomercials, I have these observations. The Ginsu knives will slice through a bowling shoe, but is that what you're cutting up in the kitchen? Food dehydrators are great, but do you know how long it would take me to eat six pounds of beef jerky? Even if I did, do you know what it's like to have to floss with a 50 pound fishing line? What about those tapes on how to stop putting things off — will folks who need them really pick up their phone and call *right* now? What about the pills that will help you lose 20 pounds in a week? Well, that's what you'll drop chasing after the company for a refund. Infomercials are akin to a markedly obese motivational speaker telling me how to accomplish goals, or a physician who smokes telling me the dangers of tar and nicotine.

Let me ask you this, how would you feel about taking a time management seminar from a presenter who showed up late, or someone who promised to give you tips on procrastination as soon as they get around to writing them down? We need to put a little more emphasis on actions and a little less emphasis on talk.

I believe it was Chapin who said, "Every action in our lives touches on some chord that will vibrate in eternity." Now, I'm not saying people don't sometimes make mistakes and then learn from them, but when someone exerts the same behavior over and over again, I think we have a pattern here, and it doesn't take The Amazing Kreskin to figure out what the next behavior is going to be. Because of that, here is a conversation that I would like to hear a lot more often:

Defendant: "Your Honor, I know this is the seventh time I've been caught robbing a convenience store, but I promise never to do it again."

Judge: "Wrong answer, but thank you for playing. Go directly to jail, do not pass Go, do not collect $200. You can't have your freedom until you prove to me you're going to be good."

Chapter 19

Go Ask Your Dad

•
Commitment
•

There is an art form in determining which parent to ask. As a kid, I always thought of my parents as a professional wrestling tag team. You don't want both of them in the ring at the same time. You can usually handle either one of them separately, but together you could expect a verbal full Nelson on your idea. And you wanted a "yes" immediately, because the longer the delay the greater the risk of not getting your way. It's similar to asking someone for a date. Usually that long delay between your asking and her answering is not a good sign. She is not delaying because she can't figure out how to tell you you're more irresistible than a fudge brownie. No, that long pause probably means you're going to hear something like, "I'd like to go out with you, but that's the night I always groom my gerbil."

You want an answer quickly. If one parent waivers, then they seek back up and suggest you ask the other parent. The other parent is suspicious because parent #1 questioned the activity. Then parent #2 doesn't want to overlook something important, so they become more suspicious than normal. It's very confusing. Trying to out guess your parents is a low percentage guessing game of chess. One wrong move and you're sitting in your room with two pawns and a castle. Now, I don't know how to play chess, but I do know the pawns and the castle aren't the big prizes.

Generally speaking, I would ask my Mom for stuff because as the oldest son, I could get away with more. There's a special connection between a Mom and her oldest son. That's why I think Mom liked me best. That was until my brother got her front-row seats to a Johnny Mathis concert. I've been second fiddle ever since. But it's time for my comeuppance. I've put her on the cover of my book. Hah! Top that one, bro.

When Mom said, "Go ask your Dad," she wanted to see what our level of commitment was. If we were willing to go the extra step and approach Dad, then it must be important because asking Dad was no easy task. My Dad wasn't mean or unloving, he was just a little distant and stern, and expected us to be responsible. I was 18 before I realized my name was not "Get Wood" (old joke, but it works really well here). Dad was the ultimate authority figure — he made a Supreme Court judge look like a notary public. If you were going to ask him for something, it had to be important.

A lot we do needs a higher commitment level. Too often we do things halfway. This is not true with my brother Jay. When he takes on a project he is the embodiment of commitment and focus. Coaching his son's basketball team, buying a car, or building his kids a playground set all take on the importance of nuclear war. There is no going halfway for him. He believes in that acronym DIRT FEET. Do It Right The First-time, Each and Every Time. As a child, he was the opposite of this. He was so laid back and indifferent, we thought he was the Beverly Hillbillies' bloodhound reincarnated. He would sleep until noon, get up to eat, and then go back to bed. But those days are the distant past. He apparently was just resting up. He is now one of the most focused, intense, committed men I've ever seen.

We need more people like Jay, who are totally committed. I want the maintenance guy working on the airplane to be totally committed to his job. I want the lady putting the raisins in the Raisin Bran to make sure there are at least two scoops in every box. And I want that guy at the fast food joint making my hamburger to even out the catsup and put the pickle in the middle. I don't want to hear by barber say "Whoops!" And I don't want my lawyer to ask me, "Are we the party of the first part or is that them other guys?" We've all heard it before, if it's worth doing, it's worth doing right. No half-hearted effort is what I'm talking about. I want commitment all the way.

Before you take on the task, ask yourself a simple question. "Am I willing to carry this through to the end, or am I going to abandon ship the first time we spring a leak?" We've got too many people jumping ship just because things didn't go like they had planned. These are the people who would have run away from home as a kid, but didn't because no one helped them pack. Sometimes we put our best foot forward, then drag the other one. The first step in any project is commitment. Total commitment, both feet. It's like that old ham-and-egg breakfast joke — the chicken was involved, the pig was committed.

As a child, commitments are forced on you by your parents. For example, they made you practice the piano and brush your teeth. (Hopefully not at the same time, you don't see many pianos in the bathroom.) As you get older you see that both of those commitments were in your best interest, because today you can play a mean Mozart and you still have your molars. Commitment means taking the good and the bad. It means taking the credit for the great party you had last night if you can also take credit for cleaning the house yesterday afternoon. It means gladly accepting the congratulations for your daughter's victory in the spelling bee if you also spent hours drilling her on the tough words.

Here are some simple commitment questions:

1) Have you logged more miles walking around that treadmill in your bedroom than on it?

2) Do you treat your car the same way you did when you bought it, or do you treat it like a rental?

3) Are your barbells dusty?

4) When you're painting the house, does the first half look like the work of a Michaelangelo and the second half like a Stevie Wonder?

5) Does the second week of your diet look like an all-you-can-eat buffet?

6) The last time you moved, did you consider your work done after you mailed your new address to TV Guide?

7) Was the last exercise in your workout lighting the grill?

If you answered yes to any of these, then you probably floss frequently right after your dental checkup and within two weeks you only floss during an eclipse. Should you do that? I don't know. Go ask your Dad.

Chapter 20

You Can't Have Dessert Until You Clean Your Plate

••••••••••••••••••••••••••

Paying Dues

••••••••••••••••••••••••••

Maybe because we were poor, or because there were starving people in underdeveloped countries, or maybe Mom just wanted to make doing dishes easier; whatever the reason, we didn't get dessert until we cleaned our plates. Mom really liked that line about the children starving in China. Once, when Mom served boiled okra — I hate boiled okra because I hate anything that swallows faster than I do — I whined, "Mom, I don't want to eat this." Of course, she reminded me right at that moment there were starving children in China. And I said, "So, they have your boiled okra recipe there, too, huh?"

Mom was adamant about cleaning the plate — fork-scraping, bread-wiping, juice-slurping clean. Skipping dessert was not a price you wanted to pay for leaving food on the plate. Mom's desserts were not to be skipped, because they were the ultimate — from apple pie to the world's greatest custard — you didn't skip Mom's desserts. That was a different era, wasn't it? Nobody worried about fat, sugar, or their cholesterol levels. You had a fried chicken dinner with fried potatoes, bread slathered with butter, then topped it off with homemade pie covered with real ice cream. If you'd been listening while you ate, you could have heard your arteries snapping shut. But to get that dessert, you had to clean your plate of every small morsel from cauliflower to mystery meat (she still won't say what it was). It had to be gone. We devised many ways to get our plates clean. We would send Mom back into the kitchen on a bogus bread run so we could scrape what we didn't eat back into the serving bowl. You could play football with Mom's mashed potatoes. We'd sneak them to the dog when she wasn't looking. These were tricks we used to get dessert. I think Mom could tell we wanted her out of the dining room because we'd say things like, "Mom, while you're in the kitchen getting that bread maybe you ought to clean that oven!"

Now, I don't know a lot about food and nutrition, but I do know that desserts are the best part of eating. Oh, I know obvious things, like you shouldn't buy anything in the meat case that is hunter green; or buy anything in a package that is covered with clowns; and you shouldn't choose foods with an expiration date that reads: "Best if eaten before the Second Coming." Despite my limited dietary knowledge, I know that the two ingredients necessary for good flavor are fat and sugar. This is why we don't want to lose our dessert. It has stuff that tastes good . . . fat and sugar.

Mom was trying to get us to see the dessert as a reward. You pay your dues and then you get the reward. Too many people today don't want to pay their dues. They just want the good stuff now. "I'm not going to do anything to deserve this, but I want a million bucks now!" I think this is the philosophy that drives the lottery. Why would you want to be a lottery winner anyway? You have friends and relatives rushing out of the woodwork clamoring for their share. Hey, I just got them to stop calling and bugging me, if I won the lottery I'd never get rid of them. You also have demands for every donation under the sun. Is "People Suffering Woodworking Withdrawal Symptoms" a legitimate charitable organization? Winning the lottery apparently lowers your intelligence too. All the lottery winners I've ever seen on television act like they barely have the skills to dress themselves. "I've just won the lottery and the first thing I'm going to do is put new skirting on the trailer home." Hey, Goober, forget the skirting and buy a new home.

I've always believed that the lottery was voluntary taxation for people who are very bad at math. Here's a novel concept instead: pay your dues, work hard, live within your means, invest wisely, and you'll be a millionaire.

Those correspondence schools advertised on TV that allow you to get your degree in weeks, run against the grain of paying your dues. I've often wondered, if you have a graduation party when you finish correspondence school, should you invite your mailman? And where do you have your senior prom? At the post office?

Listen up folks, if it's worth having, it will take some time to get. This applies to money, relationships, careers, degrees, or anything else. We live in an instant gratification society.

Everybody wants the good stuff now. We don't want to pay any price to get it. We need to remember that old quote, "the only place you find success before work is in the dictionary." With few exceptions, those people who are successful became so by paying their dues. So don't ignore the fact that they may have saved, scraped, and sacrificed.

Sacrifice. Now there's a word you don't hear too often anymore. Of course, Mom and Dad were experts at sacrificing. We always heard a new story about the hard life they had after they said those magic words, "When I was your age." "We didn't have color TV, or a VCR. We had an old radio in the living room and our clothes were so ragged we would whistle in the wind. And we had to walk to school five miles . . . uphill . . . both ways."

Let's be fair. When we talk to our kids about making sacrifices, does it make a big impression? "When I was your age, we had to walk a mile in the snow to get to the ski lift." Or, "When I was your age, it was tough — our TV didn't have a remote control. I had to get up out of the Lazy Boy Recliner and walk all the way across the living room to change channels."

From time to time we all want it now. We want to skip paying the dues. We want the dessert now. That's when we need to remind ourselves that the footprints of successful people in the sands of time are wearing work shoes. And the world does not owe you a living. The world was here first.

It would be nice if there was an abundance of everything good and pleasurable. But there's not. That's why we need to pay our dues, put in the grunt work, sacrifice a little, and clean our plates before we can have that dessert. It'll taste much better if we do.

Chapter 21

Look Both Ways Before Crossing The Street

•
Patience
•

A rhinoceros can look two ways at one time because their eyes are on the side of their heads. They can look left and right at the same time. This is a very handy trait when crossing the street, which is why you hardly ever see a rhino hit by a car. Rhinos are also yielded to the same as a driver wearing a helmet, a flak jacket, and having an angry conversation with his rear-view mirror.

The downside to rhinos having eyes on the side of their heads is that they can hardly see anything in front of them. They're nearly blind to anything directly in front of them. This explains why they're always stubbing their toes. If you ever had a pet rhino, you know what I mean.

For a long time, I figured Mom thought I was a rhinoceros. When Mom would say, "Look both ways," I thought she meant simultaneously. It's virtually impossible to look both ways at the same time. You can get a severe headache trying. Looking both ways simultaneously would require humans to have heads like rhinos. That would not be an attractive thing and would create the need for radically redesigned eyewear. And no one would be able to know who or what you were looking at. You would just be looking. At everything. Stubbing your toes. I think you get the picture.

Looking both ways was one of those parental sayings that made no sense. You know the ones I'm talking about. Remember when a parent asked that brilliant question, "Do you want a spanking?" "Sure Dad, that's what I live for." Or how about that mind bender, "Who do you think you are?" "Mom, if you don't know, we need to have a long talk."

Mom didn't plan on us having rhino heads, and she didn't plan on us looking both ways at the same time. She just wanted us to take our time, look one way, then look the other way. She wanted us to make haste slowly. Mom believed patience was power. We are often in such a hurry we forget about details; we forget about looking the other way for hazards. We just want to get on with it and cross the street. We get away with it because some of the streets in life are one way, and all we need to do is look one way.

But not all the streets in life are one way. There are lots of turns, detours, and hazards along the way. We need to take our time, *slow* down, and be sure before we proceed. Count to ten before you spout that snappy sarcastic comeback.

Consider having your hair cut someplace other than a place called "Mohawks-R-Us." Look in a book of names before you label your newborn "Butterbean." Quit trying to squeeze a few extra seconds out of that stoplight and wait for the next one. So what if you get to the supermarket 30 seconds quicker, you'll still end up behind that guy trying to cash a check on the Bank of Borneo. Why do you want to get to the doctor's office early anyway and sit in that gown that would make a stripper blush? If you do need to get there quicker, here's an idea: Leave the house one stop light sooner. Take your time. Slow down. It's important. Ralph Waldo Emerson said, "Adopt the pace of nature, her secret is patience." Although patience is sometimes bitter, the fruit of patience is sweet.

Why does everything have to be so quick? I don't want eyeglasses in about an hour or dentures in a day. These things are important. Take your time. What's next? Your gall bladder removed in an hour. Hey, I want my oil changed in 15 minutes, not my vital organs. I don't want medicine in a hurry, they might forget something. We don't need a drive-in plastic surgery clinic called the "Toot and Tuck" or a drive-in dental clinic called "Park and Pull."

Everything we do is so speeded up . . . we're all in such a hurry. We're all trying to do too much at once. Yesterday a guy drove by me who was shaving and talking on his cell phone at the same time. I guess he was steering with his knees. Normally I don't mind when I see a driver shaving . . . but ladies, not your legs.

Take your time. Get it right. Exhibit a little patience and look both ways before you cross the street. Otherwise, you might get run over . . . by a rhino . . . because he can't see you.

Chapter 22

Stop Walking So Loud

••••••••••••••••••••••••

Consideration

••••••••••••••••••••••••

Clomp, Clomp, Clomp. Kids walk loud. A fact that was emphasized in our house by the lack of carpet. It was impossible to sneak up on anybody. It was like wearing cowbells — you always knew where everyone was because you could hear them coming and going. I'm convinced this was part of Mom's master plan to know when we got home at night. There was no sneaking in the house after curfew because we had to walk by Mom and Dad's bedroom. Clomp, Clomp, Clomp! "Mark, do you know what time it is?" "Sorry, Mom, what are you saying, I can't hear you; I'm making too much noise on these floors."

Even pets made a noise on those floors. I remember lying on the couch right after my appendectomy. Our pet terrier dog (who loved to lay on human stomachs) came running across the floor — pitter patter, pitter patter, pitter patter (that's a dog's version of clomp, clomp, clomp). He was preparing to leap on my recovering belly. He leapt and landed on the incision. He then flew across the room.

Our hardwood and linoleum floors amplified every step, so Mom was always saying, "Stop walking so loud." That sounds like a mixed up sentence, like "turn the radio down so I can drive." But we knew what it meant. Loud walking gets on your nerves; it's like the ticking of a clock that keeps you awake during the night: clomp, clomp, clomp . . . tick, tick, tick. Same noise, just different decibels. Mom wanted us to realize we had to be considerate of other people. Most people have forgotten the loud walking rule because consideration for others is a lost art. We clearly live in a "me-first" age.

I'm amazed when people get on an airplane with bags, buggies, suitcases, and all sorts of stuff that should've been checked. Instead of putting it underneath the seat in front of them, they monopolize the overhead bin space as though they were the only ones for which those bins were made. Come on people, this plane seats over a hundred and fifty individuals, what if all of them were that inconsiderate? Here's my idea — what we bring on the plane should be something the *average* person could carry on as opposed to what Arnold Schwarzenegger could carry on. If you can't carry it, it's not a carry-on! Duh! If you have to put wheels on the thing to drag it around because it's so heavy or so big, it's not a carry on. Check that luggage, you bonehead. The overhead bin space is for carry-on, not roll-on or drag-on. I once was in the aisle of an airplane behind a lady whose suitcase was so large it not only had wheels, it should've had license plates. And I was in one of those moods. She said: "I'm not sure which seat is mine." I said, "Well, when you get there, will you turn your blinkers on." Then she asked me to help her lift this behemoth bag. "I would," I said, "But they made me check my forklift." You know what's scary? If they're carrying on these suitcases that double as a casket, how big is the stuff that they're checking?

Consideration is just kindness. It means giving more than your share. Life is not a fifty-fifty proposition, and if you don't believe that, you don't understand fractions *or* relationships. Remember, too, that consideration and kindness is contagious. Even old Ben Franklin said, "He that has done you a kindness will be more ready to do you another."

Lack of consideration is probably most evident in lines. When someone gets to the front of the line they forget there are people behind them. Now how does this happen? Weren't they just in the line a minute ago. Now they have no consideration for the people behind them. They will ask for price checks on 59-cent items, try to cash a three-party check from El Salvador, and completely forget that anyone is waiting behind them. And most of these people get in the supermarket checkout line under the sign that reads: 15 items or less. This sign is printed in letters that are big enough to see from space, and they've got enough groceries for the next trip to Mt. Everest. I always pick the line that is the slowest moving — because it's filled with these inconsiderate yahoos. At the ATM machine, the guy in front of me is apparently trying to execute a hostile takeover of Chrysler. He hits those numbers 14 or 15 times and is there forever.

At the airline ticket counter, the bozo in front of me is trying to get to Siberia by cashing in a free ticket from another airline that routes through Kalamazoo. He's asking the agent what shots he'll need and whether customs will let him back into the country wearing a ski mask made of yak wool. I'm carrying a toothbrush and an extra shirt, and this guy is planning a voyage that would make the astronauts look like shut-ins.

At the bank drive-through, that inconsiderate fool in front of me had nothing prepared. So he sends the tube back to get a pen, then back for a deposit slip, then a calculator, and finally informs the teller she forgot his free sucker. I see the sucker, he's right in front of me. The line next to me looks like the Indianapolis 500 time trials — they're rolling through so fast, the bank has to send a clerk out carrying a checkered flag. All I'm asking, people, is to show a little consideration. Look behind you. And imagine what it would be like to be in their shoes. And speaking of shoes, stop walking so loud.

Chapter 23

Go Clean Out Your Closet

● ●

Closure

● ●

My Mom knew that people are pack rats. We collect and hoard things. We do this because we can't throw it away. After all, there's nothing wrong with it — it's just like new. Attics are filled, basements runneth over, shelves are stocked. We're saving it because we may need it someday. We want to be ready when 8-track tapes and vinyl records make their comeback. In America, we created a phenomenon in an attempt to force us to discard. This folly is known as the garage sale. Entire neighborhoods organize and host them as one huge garage sale so we can purge, sell, and barter our junk. But this doesn't work . . . because a garage sale is simply the process by which we pay for the junk in someone else's basement to become the junk in our attic. We find more junk. We make more junk. Sometimes, we even go next door to our *neighbor's* garage sale and buy his junk. He appreciates this because if he decides later that he does really need it, it's close by.

If you're wondering whether you are a junk-a-holic or a pack rat, ask yourself this question: In each of your last three moves, have you moved boxes that were never opened after the previous move? In my last move I opened one of these boxes that never gets opened. I had moved it three times and wondered what was in there. I found a broken Crock-Pot. Why did I keep this? What was I thinking? Oh, sure, a lot of men I know get bored on a Saturday afternoon and retire to the workbench to fix kitchen appliances. One could legitimately ask why would I even own a Crock-pot, let alone a broken Crock-pot. I don't cook. I only nuke things or grill things. Nuking satisfies the need for speed and men will grill because danger is involved.

In my move I also found a box of boxes. A true sign of pack rat insanity. I've thought about this. Since boxes are just containers, I was actually storing and moving air. I was collecting and saving air, just in case I might need it some day . . . you never know.

Mom wanted me to occasionally get rid of my junk. She tried to teach me the lesson of purging or closure, by getting me to clean out my closet. This is one of the most difficult tasks in life. I've decided that if you've worn an article of clothing, you apparently develop a bond to that fabric that makes it virtually impossible to discard. Intellectually, you know that the baby blue leisure suit and black patent platform shoes are artifacts for the trash heap — but emotionally, you can't give them up. They don't look good — they never did. Perhaps we should never have bought them in the first place. We wouldn't have if there had been some clothing police present.

Now, I'm not for bigger government, but obviously we need a state or federal enforcement agency that keeps us from making very bad fashion judgments. These people could also issue fines for anyone publicly violating good clothing sense. I know a lot of men that should get a *tank top ticket*. We used to call them "muscle shirts." If you have no muscles, it would make sense to me that you shouldn't wear a "muscle shirt." I don't wear a bra for the same reason, nor do my daughters wear jock straps. It's not that hard to figure out.

Issuing an occasional *Spandex summons* would be a good idea. In most cases, Spandex does not enhance your appearance. In fact, it exaggerates, or exploits your flaws. I wonder if these Spandex people have a mirror at home. They need to have mirrors on all four walls so they can look at all four sides of themselves like the public has to. I would also be in favor of issuing a few *shorts citations.* If you're scaring small children, you shouldn't wear shorts. And you guys at the beach wearing swim trunks that would fit comfortably in a cough drops box — stop it, now! That's more flesh than we can handle. You need more clothing, not less.

We are smothered with fashion felonies. And people need a closet cleaning. Mom wanted us to clean out our closet, but that was really a harbinger of what she really wanted us to do the rest of our lives — get rid of stuff! Let the past go! Sometimes the hardest thing about progress is letting go of the past. You must respect the past, remember it, and learn from it. But you cannot live the past. Let it go. Quit whining about the bad break you got and get over it.

A friend of mine told me of his twentieth high school reunion at which everyone was asked, "What is the strongest memory of your high school years?" One person answered how the clique always got the best parts in all the school plays. Lady, it's been 20 years, it's time for closure. Hang on to those good memories and wonderful thoughts, but get rid of the junk that's up there cluttering your mental attic. That's what Mom wanted us to clean out and get rid of. That feeling or emotion that you've stumbled over for years needs to get out of your closet.

What's bugging you from the past? What's the baggage burdening your brain? Are you still mad at your teacher because the guy next to you in typing class who cheated was named "best backspacer"? Get over it! Do you still cry yourself to sleep over the cancellation of "Charlie's Angels"? Get over it! Are you still not talking to your old roommate because she didn't return your copy of "The Partridge Family's Greatest Hits"? Get over it!

What's in that huge closet of your mind that just doesn't fit anymore? Are there any out-of-date ideas or beliefs or prejudices? We keep too much of the wrong stuff up there. It accumulates and eventually our closet is busting at the seams. So take a good look in there. If you haven't worn it in two years, you're not going to. Styles don't come back that much . . . and even if they did, our rear ends are probably too big anyway. So get over it. Get rid of it. And clean out your closet.

Chapter 24

There Is No Running In The House

Rules

In "Forest Gump," the movie's name sake once started running and kept running just for the sake of it. Part of the reason Forest ran was the kid in him. Kids like to run. It's not that they're in a hurry, because most of the time they're not. Now, kids don't run everywhere of course. You'll never see a kid running down the street to the dentist's office, or upstairs to bed. But most of the time they'll run, because running is cool. Running in the house is cooler. It's an obstacle course, especially on slick floors with no footing. Spinning out on corners, sliding stops, and making like cartoon characters where your feet move and your body doesn't is just flat fun. Mom should have appreciated the pitter-patter of little feet, because when it stops, one knows they are up to something. Still, running in the house was against the rules. Mom knew that uncoordinated, clumsy child bodies were disasters waiting to happen. Kids think they are bullet-proof. That's why running and jumping doesn't scare them. This brazen attitude allows kids to learn to walk and run, even though from an engineering standpoint, it should be impossible. When children are learning to walk, their bodies are half head. There is no way they should be able to learn to walk, being that top-heavy. Put a pumpkin on a pencil to get the picture. It's amazing that kids ever learn to walk and run. But they do because they don't believe they can hurt or break anything.

But this is where Mom was right. I broke lots of things in the house by running. On one cold winter day when my brothers and I were suffering from cabin fever, we turned the family room into a baseball field. The ball and bat were a ping-pong ball and paddle. The bases were pieces of furniture. While running the bases, disasters happened. We had to reattach a leg to the couch and glue light fixtures back together. Mom never knew. She does now, if she's reading this chapter. Sorry, Mom.

No running in the house. The same way, there was no bungee cord jumping off the step ladder, or scuba diving in the bathtub. These were the rules. Rules we didn't understand. Rules that invoked that one-word child response, that is guaranteed to drive any parent mad: "Why?"

"There is no running in the house."
"Why?"

"Because it's not safe."

"Why?"

"Because you could hurt yourself."

"Why?"

"Because I said so."

"Why?"

"Just because."

This could last for days if you would let it. I don't know how I got so lucky, but my daughters never really questioned the rules that much. Generally, they were rule followers. When Leah was 10 she told me she had become a *real woman* because she had received her own library card. When Lindsay was 9 she told me that the following year she was going to wear a "practice" bra (apparently similar to training). Both girls just assumed it was a rule that at age 10 you moved to adulthood.

I, on the other hand, fought the rules as a kid. I know now that the running rule was for my own good, even though I hated it. It removed some of the fun from my youth, but surely saved a lot of money and bodily harm. Mom had more rules that were for our own good, which we weren't crazy about either. In winter, we'd get so bundled to go outside that we looked like a serial shop lifter at the Burlington Coat Factory. Then there was washing behind our ears. Tell me, have you ever had a job interview where they said, "Bill, this is a great résumé, now let's take a look behind your ears." Another rule was no sitting on the good furniture. Why was cousin Leo, the one who scratched himself in places you never thought of, allowed to sit on it, but you weren't? These were just the rules. There are lots of rules in life like that.

These rules are essential to a civilized society, for the simple reason we may not be good judges ourselves and we need restrictions. Now I know some of these rules can be a nuisance but we still need them. Speed limits can be a pain, but we need them. I personally don't understand most of the rules about airline travel, but we need them. I do wonder why can't we all pay the same airfare on the plane if we're going to the same place. It works for bus travel. You don't dare ask what that person next to you paid for their airline ticket. Last time I did, I found out I paid $900 for my ticket and the guy next to me got his for three chickens and a goat. Also, I'm the only person that doesn't get to pre-board. Children, elderly people, frequent flyers, people wearing pink can all pre-board. The tray table always has to be in an upright and locked position during take-off and landing, too. I'm not so sure, but if we're going down, I don't think bumping the edge of a plastic table is one of my major concerns.

And why does it cost money to *not* have your name in the phone book? Why can the phone company charge you for *not* doing something? Based on this rule I have some advice for the phone company. Announce to all your customers that you're *not* putting them in the phone book and don't print a phone book. That will increase your bottom line by a few hundred million dollars, I guess.

And why do I have to shake my medicine before I take it? Why can't I take it and then head right for my kids' trampoline? Why? Because these are the rules. I don't like them, but I abide by them. There are, however, intelligence-challenged individuals who say when we begin to modify our freedoms we then start moving down the road to eliminating our freedoms. Not true, and in reality these people don't care about anyone's freedoms. They have selfish interests in mind, or they're muddled thinkers. Or both.

Folks, we can impose speeding limits and still allow you to drive your car. We can deny an AK-47 automatic rifle to a citizen and still honor his or her rights to bear arms. We can eliminate smoking in public places, but still let you light up at home. We can forbid the sale of dangerous substances, but still allow you to buy Spam. We can have laws against people being disorderly in public, but we can still allow you to play professional hockey or attend K-Mart sidewalk sales. We can live with rules without sacrificing our freedoms.

We could be refused the right to run in the house, but allowed to run all we wanted to outside. Rules and restrictions do not eliminate freedoms.

I have the right to swing my fist, but my right stops at the end of your nose. I can disagree with your political views, but that doesn't give me the right to put your bumper sticker over your mouth.

Sometimes we have to throw out our selfish interests and accept general standards and rules that are for the good of the group. Maturity is the ability to operate in someone else's world. So accept a few rules that you don't like. Accept a few rules that you haven't authored and stop running in the house.

Chapter 25

Stop Running With Those Scissors

●●●●●●●●●●●●●●●●●●●●●●●●
Safety
●●●●●●●●●●●●●●●●●●●●●●●●

Getting caught running with scissors would get one of the loudest shouts from Mom. She wanted to make sure we heard this rule. It would be followed with something like, "You could put an eye out!" This rule often involved an explanation like, "It's just not safe to combine running and sharp instruments." No more than it's smart to combine swimming and electrical repair, or driving and eyebrow plucking. This was Mom's way of saying "better safe than sorry." Her first lesson in safety was about the scissors and she hammered it into us.

Mom had to harp at the issue of safety because farm boys are notorious daredevils. Even with her efforts we still pulled off some really unsafe (okay, stupid) stunts. We jumped off the roof of the house into a snowdrift, or swam in a snake-infested pond, or played army by throwing rocks at each other from short distances. And just to show you how we really risked our lives, we "accidentally" walked in on our older sister taking a bath. I can't imagine what risks we would have taken without Mom's reminders. She would've been saying, "Stop running with that chain saw." But for some reason, most moms use the scissors warning. Why is that? Did you ever meet anyone who put his eye out that way? Come to think of it, I never heard of anyone who put his eye out with a BB gun either, but there must be a kid somewhere. When are the TV people going to look for him on "Unsolved Mysteries?" I just realized Mom's ultimate nightmare — seeing me running with a pair of scissors toward my brother who's shooting his BB gun. Now that's scary.

Kids don't understand this safety thing until they become parents themselves. Then they hope their kids never do the things they did, and that they are more safe than they were. But I look around all the time and see this doesn't happen. We drive too fast, we eat too poorly, we smoke too much, we drink in excess — we just aren't safe. Here are some of my rules of safety we should all follow:

1) Never follow a car closer than where you think your Grandpa on Prozac could stop in time.

2) Never drink to the point that you tell a guy named Bubba he has a stupid name.

3) Never get in a taxi numbered "666."

4) Don't drink milk you have to stir.

5) Don't try to pet a dog chewing on a human leg.

6) Don't call a policeman "Barney."

7) Don't ask Mike Tyson if he wants to go out and get a bite.

8) Don't fly on any airline that has the word "maybe" in its name.

9) Don't believe the weatherman . . . ever!

10) Don't skydive, bungee jump, hang glide, or climb Mt. McKinley. The key concept here is gravity.

We just do a lot of unsafe stuff. We even have unsafe sporting events. That NASCAR race sponsored by Budweiser. Is this a good marriage of concepts? Don't we know the perils of drinking and driving? What about the Virginia Slims tennis tournament? How did exercise and smoking become linked together? What's next? The "All Bran Marathon," or the "Preparation H Tour de France Bicycle Race"? I saw a product advertised in a catalog that I thought was very unsafe: A radio for your shower. Is this a good place to dance? Slick floor, glass door, think about it.

There's enough danger in this world that we have no control over. It starts at birth and we are forced to dodge danger our entire lives. Why do we want to subject ourselves to more danger by being unsafe? Now, I'm not advocating that we lead sheltered, unexciting lives, free of all risks. I've even included a chapter about the value and importance of risk-taking. But I'm talking about the silly, unsafe stuff we do. Being safe isn't that hard, it just means we have to be smart. Okay, I take that back. We seem to do more stupid, a.k.a. unsafe stuff, all the time. Surely you heard about the crook who entered a record store in Michigan and yelled, "Nobody move!" When his partner moved, he shot him. Did you hear about the driver who thought cruise control was like an autopilot function? He set the cruise, reclined his seat, and began to doze off. He went off the road and hit a tree. Ages ago, these people would not have survived; they would have been eaten by saber-tooth tigers. The dumb ones used to die. Now they live and do careless acts like this. They personify what is going on everywhere.

We need to practice that slogan "Safety First." *Drink in moderation.* If you've ever awakened wearing someone else's trousers, it's time to cut back on the booze. *Slow down.* This especially applies if you ever received a speeding ticket . . . while driving in reverse. *Stop smoking.* Particularly if you run out of breath while buttoning your cuffs. *Get enough sleep.* Especially if you catch yourself falling asleep during breakfast, before lunch, and while waiting for the fireman to arrive. *Eat right.* This is for those of you who have valet parking at McDonald's. Don't blow-dry your hair in the bathtub! Don't shovel snow in the nude! And stop running with those scissors!

Chapter 26

Speak When You're Spoken To

· ·

Tact

· ·

"Sit there and don't say a word." "Speak when you're spoken to!" We've all heard these things a time or two, haven't we? At our household this rule surfaced when someone said something they shouldn't have, like telling Mom that Dad said her gravy could be used for wallpaper paste. Or sharing with the mailman that Mommy didn't wear panties to bed. Those were snippets that landed me speechless on the couch. Of course, parents who use this phrase often confuse their kids about whether they're supposed to keep quiet. The confusion for me usually followed a statement from Mom that went something like this: "You just sit there and don't say a word. Now, why did you put marshmallow creme in your brother's ears?" What do I do? Sit here and don't say a word, or answer her question?

Mom was trying to impart a simple lesson: tact. Occasionally we need to sugar-coat our emotions or just not say anything at all. Mom said we do this out of respect for other people's feelings. Mom knew there were some things nobody wants or needs to hear about. These certainly include a detailed discussion of your brother's bathing habits, or lack thereof; your latest root canal; or what the inside of a frog looks like.

Tact is making a point without making an enemy. And occasionally it does mean saying nothing. We all know how to say nothing but few of us know when. Tact is sometimes the ability to close your mouth before someone else does. You want to respond to that tongue-in-cheek accusation from your mother-in-law, but don't do it. Bite your lip. This is not the time. I know you want to tell your supervisor to take that project and place it where there is a lack of sunshine, but cork your pie hole and keep quiet, it's not your turn to speak. You'll often find out by waiting, the urge will go away, and you won't end up eating filet of "rubber" sole.

Actually, the old rule is still a good one. Count to ten before you say anything. In fact — and this is important — be sure to stop at ten. I find that if I count to more than ten, all I've done is give myself more time to come up with an even nastier remark.

I once stormed into my golf club house and began ranting to my friend, the head golf professional, about an old man in front of me on the golf course who was incredibly slow and irritating. I said he had no business being on the golf course because he was too old, he was a bad player, and he was slowing up play. I asked the pro if he had any idea who this *fool* was. He told me, "Yes, it's my Dad." I'll take a little salt with those sneakers, thank you.

Or what about the editor of a college newspaper who had a staff member bring in an extreme close-up photo of the face of a very old, wrinkled man. The staffer, obviously proud of his work, asked the editor, "What do you think of these pictures?" "Good grief," the editor said, "What is this, an old leather boot with eyes?" "No," the staffer said, "he's my Grandfather."

Just remember, unkind remarks aren't like a fishing line. Once you throw them out, you can't reel them back in. If you've been shooting your mouth off faster than Fourth of July fireworks, you probably don't realize how quickly your listeners tune you out. But a funny thing happens to folks who are quiet most of the time — once they do talk, they get more attention than Wally or Wilma Windbag. Which reminds me of a phrase an old school teacher of mine used to say, "Quiet people aren't the only ones who don't say much." In other words, a lot of quiet people ought to talk more and a lot of talkative people ought to be quiet more.

Are you the guy who shouts to the referee at the ball game from 100 yards away? Do you yell at the television set when someone on the TV says something you don't agree with? Is jumping into an argument your idea of good conversation? A "yes" answer to any of these may mean you need to practice a little tact and zip it up.

When the guy who says your car is blocking his looks like he could move a refrigerator by putting it under his arm, zip it up.

When the slow foursome ahead of you on the golf course includes your boss, your boss's wife, or the guy who audited your tax return for the past three years, zip it up.

If you're not sure whether you should say something in a given situation, remember, "silence is golden." When in doubt, don't speak out.

Generally speaking, you can't get in trouble for what you don't say; and who says silence can't be interesting? Have you ever seen Marcel Marceau? He has the audience hanging on his every nonword.

Practice a little tact — which is really just saying or doing the right thing at the right time to keep from offending folks. Or, as a friend of mine used to say, "It's not talking about what bait you use while I'm eating spaghetti; and it's not inviting Father O'Malley to your bachelor party."

As the old proverb goes, "It's better to keep silent and have people think you are a fool, than to open your mouth and remove all doubt."

Remember this, not everyone is quite as enamored with your voice and your opinion as you are. This is why I get so irritated with people who talk so loud in public places that everyone can hear them. They think everything they say is hilarious or profound or the truth . . . or all three. I'm sure this habit has something to do with insecurity — pretty much everything does. But we've got to do something about this. I've already recommended clothing police to ticket a fashion faux pas. I think these police could also monitor vocal violations. If you're too loud, or you're saying something stupid, they could "ticket" your tongue and "muzzle" you. We wouldn't have to endure hearing too much information about the relationship dilemma from Gossip Gary. Jabberbox Jackie would have to keep that inside scoop to herself. These people would just have to sit there and not say a word. Or at least not speak until they're spoken to.

Get Out Of Bed, You've Got Things To Do

....

Hard Work

....

I hate myself. Okay, I don't hate myself, but I'm downright frustrated with myself. When I was a kid I could have slept 20 hours a day if my Mom had let me. I would have had to fluff up my pillow *and* my box springs. If Mom would have let me, I might have slept so long that I'd wake up, look at my pajamas and say, "What happened? They fit when I went to bed."

For me, being hyperactive was falling out of bed. I could have slept late but I always had school or some activity or chores. All I know is I never got to sleep in because Mom was hollering, "Get out of bed; you've got things to do."

Mom was right, of course. You can't get anything worthwhile accomplished in bed (at least nothing you can include in a book with Mom's name on it). What I'm frustrated about is that now I get to call my own shots and I can sleep in on Saturday; why then am I lying in bed wide awake at 6:00 a.m. with no chance of going back to sleep? Why couldn't this have happened when I was 16? Mom programmed me not to sleep the day away and to do something productive. She taught me the virtue of hard work, which more of us could know. Now I don't mean to say that people have gotten lazy, let's be objective and exact. People have gotten a *lot* more lazy. The value of a good day's work isn't known or practiced enough anymore.

I've always hated people who start every conversation with "When I was a boy . . ." But if I may take a little liberty from my Grandpa . . . When I was a boy, one of the greatest attributes one could possess was the ability to put in a good day's work. Mom often quoted that "idle-time, devil's-workshop" axiom. My Grandma often assessed one's worth by saying, "She's a good worker." Except for a few segments of our economy, we don't know what hard work is anymore. In Grandpa's time getting hurt on the job meant falling at the sawmill or losing a finger at the factory. Today's employees file Worker's Comp claims for slipping in the shower in the employee gym.

Winston Churchill once made shedding "blood, sweat, and tears" sound positively noble. Today, you show me a person covered with blood, sweat, and tears and I'll show you an old boxer who just came out of retirement. Our goal today seems to be how little we can work and still get by. But deep down we all know that getting by is never good enough. And if you're a boss there's one thing you want to say to an employee who is just getting by: "good-bye." Give the boss a full day's work for a full day's pay. Don't be like the guy who said (only half in jest), "I couldn't afford to work for what I'm worth."

This hard work virtue is something I will always remember about my brother Clint. He died in an accident at the age of 13, but even at that age he could out work most grown men. His hands were always dirty because he had been working in the shop or tinkering with an engine or building something. He had so many great virtues, but none greater than his willingness to work fiercely at whatever he was doing.

I'm not advocating we return to those days of labor-intensive, health-risking, unsafe, unfair working conditions of yesteryear. But it would be nice to see people willing to sweat and toil a little bit more; to be thankful they have a job and not complain about the smallest peccadillo as a reason not to work. I'm so tired of hearing, "I just can't work in these conditions," when the conditions aren't that bad. We've spoiled everyone. We don't know what work is anymore. I hear talk about the four-day work week, I know lots of people who have a four-day work week . . . spread out over five days. What happened to the idea that it's better to wear out than to rust out? Or as my Dad used to say, "hard work never hurt anybody."

I saw a celebrity sentenced to a jail term for a drug charge recently and he was assigned to a work detail of doing laundry and washing prison vehicles. They made a big deal about the "hard labor" he was serving. Folks, please, this isn't hard labor. For most of us, doing laundry and washing cars is a weekend. For this guy, hard labor is having to ring twice for the maid. Here's more proof of this phenomenon: Drive around and look at the public work crews. Count the number of people behind the shovel and the number of people leaning on them. See what I mean?

Talk all you want about focus, creativity, belief systems, and paradigms; hard work is still the one virtue that is not replaceable. My Dad used to say that he'd gladly take a dumb, hard worker than a bright one who watches the clock. You've run into these "work-shirkers" everywhere: The checkout clerk who's asked the price of an item and says, "I don't know, do you want me to check?" I always want to say, "No, let's just wait here until January when the inventory takers come in and we can ask them."

We need to bust our rearends a little more. At your last evaluation, did your boss say, "Your raise will become effective when you do?" Leisure is a beautiful garment, but it will not do for constant wear. Remember, it's better to be bent from hard work than crooked from avoiding it. So if your nickname is "Blister" because you never appear until after the work is done, knuckle down and don't be afraid to get your hands dirty.

When was it that we started slipping? What caused the decline in good old hard work? Was it with the introduction of the TV dinner, or when Velcro started replacing buttons, or the invention of the electric hammer? No, everyone knows when this started — it was the snooze alarm. Historians and researchers can clearly tie the decline in the work ethic to the invention of this marvelous alarm feature. If you don't want to get up and get to work, fine, just hit that snooze alarm and go back to sleep. Not ready to get up ten minutes later? Fine. Hit that button again, and again, and again. Now it's too late to get to work so you call in a fake sickness, lay around all day, and become even more lethargic. The next day you can't get going either. Hit that button again. We went downhill because of that danged snooze alarm. We need to outlaw them and mandate that everyone use one of those old windup, spring-loaded, bell-ringing, eardrum-busting alarm clocks that if you don't pick it up and turn it off, it will rattle and bounce off of the headboard and smack you in the face. It'll wake you up and get you out of bed so you can get something done.

Chapter 28

Don't Eat That, It Will Spoil Your Supper

Order

Thin rule has no scientific basis.

You can tell I'm a Mid-Westerner because we call the evening meal supper, not dinner. Except on Sundays when dinner was the midday meal. Got that? Every other day of the week it was lunch, but not on Sunday. After Sunday dinner (the midday meal) what was the meal we had about 6 p.m.? We didn't call it anything. About six, when I said, "Mom, I'm hungry," she would say, "There's some pot roast left from dinner. Go ahead and make yourself a sandwich, but save enough for your lunch tomorrow." Lunch, of course, was the midday meal at school followed by . . . well, you get the idea.

But the spoil-your-dinner-rule applied to breakfast, lunch and supper, too. Mom would recite it when we went to the cookie jar an hour before any meal. How could a cookie spoil roast beef, mashed potatoes and gravy? What chemical reaction could possibly be created between these seemingly harmless foods? None. It was a scare tactic. A huge lie. There is no spoiling of the food. There! I've said it, and now the world knows. Maybe Mom wanted us so ravenous we would gulp down supper and allow her to cook literally anything (bird beak quiche) and we would think it was great. But that wasn't really the issue because nothing could spoil our dinner. I mean, we didn't just sit down at the dinner table, we landed there like the Marines on Guadalcanal. We were like locusts with silverware. My brother's fork had racing stripes.

Maybe Mom really believed that curbing a hunger pang an hour before dinner did create some fermenting process that spoiled food. Or maybe Mom wanted us to learn that there is an order to life and there is a reason for it. Which was Mom's way of saying, "Don't get the cart before the horse."

Everything has an order to it. Remember the verse that goes, "To everything there is a season . . ." (Except for the NBA; their season runs continuously apart from that one morning in August).

Men are particularly good at getting the cart before the horse. I can prove it. How many of you men have parts left over to a "self-assembly" project because you wouldn't read the directions first? Before you answer, look across the room at that computer desk that wobbles because you forgot the cross braces. You jumped in with a I-think-this-goes-here philosophy. In fact, the folks who make those "self-assembly" products should really have two sets of instructions in the package. One with step-by-step instructions and detailed pictures on how it should look. The other set of instructions would be labeled "For Men Only" and would have one picture of the assembled product with the caption, "Guys, this is what is looks like. Good luck." A second photo would include all the parts with the caption, "This is what you're supposed to use, more or less." Oh, and at the bottom of the men's instructions would be a toll-free telephone number followed by, "Guys, here's who you call to swear at when you screw things up." I have to believe that right this minute God is saying, "Verily there would be less swearing on the planet Earth if men would just read the instructions *first*."

Other than my DVR, my main TV technology is picture-in-picture. This feature is extremely valuable because it allows me to watch TV with no commercials. I deplore commercials because they insult our intelligence. They tell us things like "the best part of waking up is coffee in your cup." I don't think so. No, the best part of waking up is just waking up. If the best part of waking up for you is a cup of coffee, then your life really sucks. Anyway, when I brought my first TV with P-I-P home, I turned it on, and immediately started pushing "P-I-P" buttons. Try this . . . well then, try that. Then try this again. After fifteen minutes, I did what I should have — I read the manual. That's the order — read the TV manual, install the TV, operate the TV. I still have a VCR for playing old tapes and it still flashes 12:00 — it's because I lost the manual. In my excitement of hooking it up, I threw it away with the packing material. I forgot the order.

I had a ninth grade teacher who would write in big letters at the top of every test: WAEFRD: When All Else Fails, Read the Directions. And you know what, 99 percent of the time doing just that completely answered our questions. Of course, when you're in the ninth grade, you're lucky if you can remember how to find your classroom, let alone how to factor polynomials.

This is why I struggle with computers. I want to jump right in without first understanding the basics. I just want to do the "stuff." I don't want to learn about hard drives or software — I just want to print "stuff." Crawl before we walk is the sequence here; that's the order. Because I haven't done the steps in the right order, I am not very competent with computers. Okay, I'm completely incompetent. In my mind a megabyte is a dental deformity, and booting up the computer is done by putting my foot through the screen. I once asked a store clerk if this one particular mousepad was compatible with my computer. If you don't follow the order, you struggle with it forever.

You don't think there's an order to the universe? Have you ever heard anybody say, "First things second"?

A few years ago, on a cab ride to the airport, we had a flat tire. The cab driver didn't know how to change the tire and this was compounded by the fact he could barely speak English. Here's my thought on what should have been the proper order of this scenario. Number one, learn to speak English. Number two, learn how a vehicle operates. Number three, drive the vehicle. This is the correct sequence. You don't drive the taxi first!

If you've ever taken flying lessons you know you don't practice landings before practicing takeoffs. If you're learning to ski, they don't take you to the top of the mountain before you've mastered the bunny slopes. And you probably don't even start ski lessons until you've mastered your fear of heights (or had eight tequila kamikaze shooters, whichever comes first).

Whatever the project, there is an order to follow. Because so few people do this, if you do things in order, it will gratify some people and astonish the rest. Whether it's putting together a plant stand or earning a college degree, we walk before we run. Mess with the order and you're courting disaster.

Getting things out of sequence is akin to building a house by starting with the roof and finishing with the foundation. This is why I don't want my new car to get the paint job first. I want the undercarriage and the frame to receive attention first. (That's what my car manual said.) There is an order and a reason why. This is why the news starts with world events and ends with sports. If you started with sports, most men would turn off the TV after sports and never know what was going on in the rest of the world. You have to have sports last, just like you have to have the dessert last, otherwise it will spoil your supper.

Chapter 29

Don't Cross Your Eyes, They'll Stay That Way

Permanence

W hat is the fascination with crossing your eyes? You can't see, because everything is double. If you do it for very long, you get a headache that pounds into tomorrow. Why do kids do it? Simple . . . it's a funny face. If you don't believe that, think back to Howdy Doody, Pee Wee Herman, or Bert and Ernie. A funny face is an international form of kid humor.

That's why sticking out your tongue or sticking your thumbs in your ears and wiggling your other eight fingers is universally accepted child behavior. Same for pushing up the end of your nose for the ever popular pig-nose face. A funny face is always in vogue with a kid. But most funny faces didn't warrant the threat of "stop it, or they'll stay that way." Apparently those other faces weren't that special permanent reinforcing type of behavior that eye-crossing fell into. Mom, I guess, knew this. She never said, "stop making that pig-nose face, it'll stay that way." That's a good thing. If a pig-nose face could be permanent, pity the child that goes to the county fair with his folks. They would come home with corn dogs, he would come home with a blue ribbon. You couldn't walk in the rain without an umbrella or you would drown. And you would need a nose hair trimmer because your nose hairs would show. You'd look like my Uncle Herb, who had hair growing like wild ivy out of every facial orifice. His barber would ask "do you want me to trim those ears or braid them?" He had a turbo nose hair trimmer that boasted razor sharp stainless steel blades rotating at 500 rpm. It had three speeds: slow, medium and hold-my-feet. I've often wondered, if you had a piece of equipment with razor sharp, stainless steel blades rotating at 500 rpm, what is the first logical thing you should do with it? That's what I thought — stick it up your nose! Well anyway, because of the nose hair thing or whatever reason, it's just a good thing pig-nose faces don't stick.

Mom was only worried about the eye-crossing thing. I think she really wanted us to remember that what we do stays with us forever. We form habits early. Sometimes without even knowing it. Samuel Johnson said, "The chains of habit are too weak to be felt until they are too strong to be broken." Why is it that the good habits are easier to break than the bad ones? Every action, statement, or behavior becomes a perma-nent brand that we have with us our entire lives. I know I am branded. I will always be a farm boy. When I smell manure,

I think of home. In fact, when people ask me why I love the circus, I tell them I grew up on a farm and I miss the smell. And I was an ornery farm boy. On our farm, if you saw a cat with a tail on it, you knew he was a visitor. (That's just a joke, I love cats. . .they taste like chicken. That's another joke, I'm kidding, I really do love cats.)

I've been branded a small-town guy and it's true. I used to drag Main Street. I can name everyone in my high school graduation class. I can remember buying a pack of cigarettes in town, and by the time I got home my Mom knew about it. I am a small-town guy and that's with me forever. People form images of us, and those images change little, if any, over time. So what we say and do will last forever.

Here's a news flash. When you're a kid, if you're irritable, caustic, and have the personality of a bucket of hair, you're probably going to be that way when you draw your last breath. That's why what you are today tells me a lot about what kind of kid you were. If you're a brown nose with your boss, you probably didn't just bring your teacher an apple, you gift wrapped an apple pie. If you've written your boss a memo complaining about a co-worker, I bet you were a relentless hall monitor. And if your lawn looks like you traded your mower for a pair of manicure scissors, then I bet you're a person who polished your pocket protector as a kid.

How many people from your high school class underwent a metamorphosis from happy to grouchy or vice-versa since those adolescent days? Few if any. Our class clown, after 25 years, is still the class clown. The guy in class everyone hated because of his pompous showboat style doesn't get invited to reunions. I once heard that there were three kinds of people in the world — left handed, right handed, and underhanded. Whichever you became you started at an early age because what you do stays with you forever. These small behavioral activities or habits then become your attitudes and core beliefs that stay with you and define your life. So if you're convinced you've got no talent and no marketable skills when you're young, then you should probably plan to host a daytime talk show. If you avoided decisions and couldn't make up your mind as a child, then you should have planned a career as a TV weather forecaster. And if people seem to seek you out for advice and listen carefully to what you're saying, then you should fill out a job application for the Psychic Friends Network.

I had a Sunday School teacher one time who said, "Be pleasant until ten o'clock in the morning, and the rest of the day will take care of itself." What he was implying is what you say and what you do becomes your brand, or your logo, or, to be contemporary, your tattoo. Our actions are the tattoos that people remember forever.

Your behavior will forever remain your signature. When my daughter Lindsay was in second grade, she invited me to speak to her class on what I did for a living. For an hour I made them laugh by doing impressions, telling jokes, and answering questions. They were the best crowd I have ever had. I was "rockin' the house." Because of the rowdiness I created in the classroom, the teacher labeled them "Mayfield's Animals." They chanted "Mayfield's Animals" as they went down the hall to lunch. Years later I ran into one of Lindsay's second grade classmates who said, "Remember me? I was one of "Mayfield's Animals"? What you say and what you do stays with people . . . often forever. Remember that the next time you think about making that rude noise with your hand and armpit, or the next time you contemplate telling your prospective boss during a job interview that his wife is a fox, or when you start crossing your eyes as you look at your friend as she's presenting a proposal during a staff meeting. Stop it . . . they'll stay that way. Make the pig-nose face instead.

Chapter 30

Don't Forget To Brush Your Teeth

First Impressions

I was blessed with bad teeth that form cavities at the rate of one per Chiclet. At my death, steel companies will be fighting over the iron ore rights to my mouth. This despite the fact I brushed all the time. Maybe I brushed the enamel off. Mom was always saying, "Don't forget to brush your teeth." Not just before bedtime, she said it before I went out on a date, before I went to school, before I mowed the lawn, before I fed the dogs . . . you get the idea. It could've been worse, at least she picked something that didn't involve a lot of brains or skill. I suppose she could've said things like, "Don't forget to memorize Macbeth," or "Don't forget to spit-shine your bicycle."

Mom just wanted me to brush my teeth because she knew first impressions were often the most valuable. She knew that if your teeth looked like you'd just eaten a box of Oreos, or if your breath could change the color of someone's tie, you were doomed for failure. We used to believe that old adage: You don't have a second chance to make a first impression. Now too many of us believe we *do* have a second chance, so we don't worry about the first 30 seconds of a conversation or the first image we project. I'm as guilty as anyone I suppose. One time at a small mom-and-pop furniture store, the owner asked me if I wanted to buy a goat. How bizarre is that? What are the odds that someone is going to ask you if you'd like to buy a goat? What do you say? "No, I just got one for my birthday." I couldn't imagine why this owner would look at me and ask that question. When I got home I glanced in the mirror and saw a two-day-old beard, disheveled work clothes, and a billed cap on backwards. I looked like I could have been a goat owner. The first impression did it. When I was looking for my new family physician because my HMO or PPO or BLT, or some other acronym changed, my decision was clearly influenced by the first impression I got from the doctor; and I didn't choose the one who had a bone through his nose.

One of the things I love that my grown daughter Leah does is to call me and say she wants a "date with her Dad." We'll go to a movie or knock around the mall and she always shows her affection by holding on to my arm. People don't know we are father and daughter and the first impression they get is that I'm robbing the cradle or at least trying to impersonate Michael Douglas. Now this first impression is one Leah and I laugh about, but many first impressions have more serious consequences.

I wish more businesses would have realized that when they installed those unbearable, lengthy, impersonal voice mail options. "If you would like customer service, press 1. If you would like account information, press 2. If you would like to press 3, press 8. If you would like to speak to a real person, press 'Q' (there is no 'Q')." This impersonal voice mail has gone too far. Tell me this rumor isn't true. Tell me that when you dial 911 you won't hear, "For a murder in progress, press 2. For a kitchen grease fire, press 3." It's so easy to make a bad impression on the phone. For instance, if you're talking to me and another call comes in, don't ask me to hold until you decide if the second caller is more interesting or important than I am.

What is the first impression you make? It's the one that often lasts forever. If you don't believe it, think about how your parents or grandparents give directions to someplace: "Go about three miles past the old Johnson place that burned down in '73, then head south till you reach the big oak tree that lightning took out in '82 . . ." Their directions were impressions that were indelibly inked in their minds decades ago — and they're still there. We are no different from our parents or grandparents. That first impression does make a difference. It sets the tone for the relationship whether it's personal or business. Sometimes the first impression is the last impression. I wonder why.

What kind of first impression do you make? If you're not sure, ask yourself these questions:

1) Does your business attire look like a Mardi Gras costume?
2) Do you speak in a clear, confident voice, or do you sound like you've got a mouthful of marshmallows?
3) Is your handshake firm, or is it like grabbing Jell-O?
4) Do you look the other person in the eye, or do you act like he's the principal and you've just been caught smoking in the boys' room?

5) Is your smile genuine, or does your expression look like you spent two hours at the all-you-can-eat burrito bar?

Those first few seconds are so critical. I wonder how many individuals know that. Apparently not many. From fast-food drive-through windows to return desks at department stores, these individuals make me feel like I am imposing on them. They don't make eye contact, exchange pleasantries, exhibit personal hygiene, or have any enthusiasm — no favorable first impression.

"Courtesy costs nothing but conveys much," was drummed into me. It pleases the one who gives *and* the one who receives. It's like being twice blessed. I just want a little courtesy and a good first impression. I'm not asking for that much. I don't want that fake, over-thc-top, syrupy, exaggerated greeting either: "How are you?" "Well, I'm great! If I was any better, I'd be twins!" Shut up, Mr. Customer Service Manual Reader; you skipped the part about sincerity. All I want is normal niceness. All I want is a good first impression, because it increases the odds of favorable impressions thereafter.

All I want is for you to not forget to brush your teeth.

Chapter 31

Get Down From There Before You Fall And Hurt Yourself

. . . .
Risk Taking
. . . .

I was raised on a farm, so there was always stuff to climb — trees, barn lofts, equipment. Climbing was one thing I was good at because I was small and light enough to fool gravity. I was so small I had to jump up and down on the scale to move the arrow. My friends, who were big guys, never experienced the thrill of climbing things. They got their thrills by belly flopping in the farm pond to create tidal waves.

I climbed. I could climb to the tops of trees, which would buckle under the weight of a normal person, but with me would only sway gently. I climbed as swiftly and easily as monkeys do. I could have used this skill my entire life; but I got bigger and moved off the farm. The authorities become suspicious when you enter your apartment by climbing up the drain spout and crawling over the railing to your second floor deck. Climbing over and up things is not deemed socially acceptable when you're 40 years old and working in an office building. The only thing you want to be caught climbing is the corporate ladder.

Mom was always worried about us kids climbing. We tried to do most of the treacherous climbing out of her view. On occasion, however, she would see us and yell from the kitchen window, "Get down from there, before you fall and hurt yourself."

Before Mom planted that seed of negative thought in our minds, we felt invincible. After her statement, we didn't. We began to think that there was a possibility we could fall. Now we had to negotiate our way down without falling. Otherwise, we would be getting down *and* falling at the same time.

Mom was concerned about our health, but she also wanted us to know where the risk taking line is. I look back now and think that Mom had been watching us climb all along, and waited to yell until we reached the point where the danger exceeded the thrill. It was okay to fall, but don't get so high that you could hurt yourself. Mom was saying that there were certain activities where the risk is too great for the reward.

It's not that Mom didn't want us to take risks, or experiment, or make mistakes. Mom always felt that life was the art of drawing with an eraser. She just wanted us to realize that some risks were too great for the reward. I feel that way about many things now. The thrill of the roller coaster is not worth the risk of being sick for two hours after the ride. It's also not worth standing in line 45 minutes for a 45 second ride. While you're standing there, you have to read those warning signs that do nothing but plant thoughts in your mind. The first sign says I shouldn't ride if I'm experiencing any "neck or back pain." My back then begins to spasm. The next sign says I shouldn't be in line if I have a "nervous disorder." My head begins to twitch. By the time I get on the ride . . . I'm thinking I'm pregnant.

I also can't figure out the craze of leaping through the air. The exhilaration of the bungee cord free-fall is not worth the risk of kissing the ground at 70 mph (the "P" in mph stands for pee, as in your pants). The reward is not worth the risk of someone incorrectly measuring the cord length.

Nor will I risk climbing a 20,000 foot high mountain in minus 70 degree wind chill. When it's that cold it has to be 100 degrees hotter just to be your freezer. Chew on that popsicle for a while. Why not just open a nudist camp in northern Siberia? Or for that matter, the whole idea of parachuting puzzles me. Unless the plane's cabin is on fire, or you're actively involved in liberating a country, there is no reason to leave a plane before it lands. And what about driving a car at 200 miles per hour in a race with other guys driving cars at the same speed. Is this for guys who don't find cobra wrestling enough of a thrill?

Everything has a risk and a return. Most of us know the return, but not the risk. Ask yourself the question, "Is it worth it?" Should you seek fashion advice from Lady GaGa or Cher? Should you ask Martha Stewart what she thinks of your living room? Should you invest in a World Wrestling Federation charm school?

Many risks, however, are definitely worth taking. Owning a car is a risk, but most of us agree, one worth taking. We face the risk of taking it to the auto mechanic and having him tell us the electronic ball-bearings need replacing and that it is going to cost $318, not counting parts and labor. We take a risk when we go to the doctor as we sit on that examining table covered with deli paper. We risk embarrassment, painful examinations, and finding out bad news. But the risks of those things are worth it for the peace of mind we get when we leave the doctor's office. And don't forget, your doctor takes a huge risk every time he examines you. Despite all his skill and training, you could have the one thing he's most afraid of — no insurance.

Relationships are a risk. That person you ask for a date is taking a risk. You've decided you want to go out, but what about him or her? They don't know if you're the nicest person since Mother Theresa or whether you're a person who's been seen applauding at the end of a Brady Bunch rerun. Or maybe you're someone who gets emotional during Ice Capades. They're taking a risk with you. But as Nehru said, "The policy of being too cautious, is the greatest risk of all." Therefore, we risk potential pain and suffering with any relationship, but the potential thrill and happiness of being connected to a mate is definitely worth it.

Your friends take risks with you, too. When they invite you to a party, will you be witty, warm, and charming, or will you do your walrus impression, complete with barking sounds and pencils up your nose? Or will you pull your chair up to the buffet table? Or will you tell the hostess her backless dress would look better if she wore it backwards?

Everything is a risk. Everything is a reward. But remember the great prizes are awarded those who take the great risks. We just have to know the amount of the risk and the size of the prize. So, think about the risk and return of your actions a little more. Remember action makes more fortunes than caution. So, occasionally you do have to go out on a limb, because that's where the fruit is. You just have to know how far to go. Remember this the next time you think about going around the world in a hot air balloon. My suggestion is simple. Get down from there, before you fall and hurt yourself.

Chapter 32

Speak Up, I Can't Read Your Mind

••••••••••••••••••••••••
Expressing Feelings
••••••••••••••••••••••••

Most kids think their moms have ESP. I think most kids believe there is still an invisible umbilical cord that allows thoughts to pass between mother and child. How else can moms always know when you're lying or when you're in trouble. And my Mom knew from the second I walked in the door that I'd been up to something. Was it that Richard Kimble, "I-am-the-fugitive" look? Or the "deer-caught-in-the-headlights" look?

With Mom, of course, you were guilty until proven innocent, and you'd better have your defense strategy very well thought out, because when she started cross-examining you, she'd make F. Lee Bailey look like Gomer Pyle. Under her questioning I'd wilt like a sunflower in the Sahara. She'd soon find more holes in my story than in a box of doughnuts.

Mom didn't have ESP, she just had good interrogation techniques. Plus, we gave Mom obvious signs, the biggest of which was when we'd repeat a question. When a kid repeats a question they're getting ready to lie. "How did that beer can get in my car?" Mom knew we were buying time to craft a bogus answer. Sometimes we would say, "Gee, that's a real good question." And Mom would always snap right back with, "I know, so I expect a real good answer."

Some men still think this strategy will work and try it on their mates. "Where was I until three in the morning?" Even if you ask like you didn't understand the question, it doesn't work. They're on to us. Sometimes when we would be fumbling for an answer or an excuse, or explaining what was bothering us, Mom would look us square in the eye and say, "Speak up, I can't read your mind."

Mom wanted us to express ourselves honestly. Even though I am still a highly private person, Mom made me much better in the department of honest expression, and we all need some help in this area. It's like we just can't say anything direct and open anymore. Have we all become politicians? *"Suffice it for me to say that in this time of historic significance with regard to political correctness and sensitivity, this moment we diligently ponder is foremost in the thoughts of all people who work to secure strong interpersonal relationships and an overt pontification of those wants in an ever-changing time of uneasiness."* Huh? Did you say we need to express ourselves better? That's what I thought you said.

We give lots of information and correct answers, but no one knows what we said. The presidential candidate says he wants a running mate that is strong, reliable, and dependable.

Is he describing his perfect running mate, or a laxative? I don't mean to single them out, but when I was a lobbyist I began to figure out what a politician said and what they really meant.

Politicians Say:	What They Mean:
"I've given the issue a lot of thought, but I'm not prepared to state a definite position at this time."	My advisors haven't figured out a position that will offend no one and put me in the middle of the road.
"I won't join my opponent in a mud-slinging campaign."	I'm going to let my aides and supporters do all the dirty stuff.
"I have no interest in being my party's candidate for vice president."	Are you kidding, to get close to the White House I'd clean the monkey house at the National Zoo.

But let's be fair, politicians aren't the only people who say one thing and mean something 180 degrees different. You run into them every day, like the real estate agent who wants to show you a "fixer upper." Don't kid yourself, this place would make a contractor cry. It was recently used on a poster soliciting donations for Turkish earthquake relief. And the agent who says the next place has a full basement. Make sure that doesn't mean it's just been stocked with trout.

Or the dentist who says, "Now this might hurt a little bit." That means get ready to feel like a mortar has just gone off in your mouth.

Or the mechanic who says, "While I'm working on it, there are a couple of little things you ought to have done." That means you'll be getting an invoice total with two commas in it.

Quit the gobbledy-gook and give me some straight talk. Tell me how you feel, don't assume I know. This is why most relationships go bad.

Wife: You never said you loved me.

Husband: I assumed you knew; I'm your husband. It's my job.

Speak up, Jethro. Instead of talking, we try to watch for those signs of a relationship going bad: A hug doesn't last as long and soon turns into a handshake; a phone call isn't returned; the phone number becomes unlisted; a barbed-wire security fence appears; attack dogs are present; the quiet cocking to the trigger of a 12-gauge. You know what I'm talking about, we've all been there.

Her: I just assumed you knew I wasn't happy.

Him: How was I to know, it's still football season; we're not due to talk for another month.

Listen, air head, if you get a birthday card addressed to "occupant," you need to talk more. If your mate introduces you as "what's his name," start talking . . . *now*!

I was always told the best time to tell your partner you loved them was before someone else did. Sometimes I think we are afraid to express ourselves because it will sound weak or insecure or possessive or something revealing. That's especially true for guys. Most of the time we're so concerned with being 110 percent male, we end up being 110 percent noncommunicative. Come on guys, admit it . . . when it comes to expressing how we really think and feel, we make a mime look like Howard Cosell. What guys really need, especially when it comes to expressing ourselves to women, is to let our hearts rule, not our hormones. So go ahead, open up once in a while, take your feelings and emotions out of the deep freeze. When they thaw out you'll be surprised how warm they make you feel.

Sometimes I think we're afraid to express ourselves because we're concerned that we won't choose the right words. You know, we try to sound knowledgeable or cool, then use a word that sounds like the one we want, but it is the wrong word. I call this verbal dyslexia. I have a friend who does this all the time. He's like a Norm Crosby wannabe. He goes to the pharmacy to get his "subscription" filled. And recently couldn't find a genuine leather coat he liked, so he bought one that was "stimulated" leather. He sends his taxes to the "Infernal Revenue Service." He has a friend whose pet was a former police dog. He tells me they used to use the dog at airports to sniff out "neurotics." His best misplacement, though, was after his vasectomy when he told me his "tentacles" had swollen. He apparently had become an octopus. I should have known, he was leaking ink.

We need to show moxie and express ourselves more. This is one of the reasons I like cats. You know exactly how a cat is feeling. If they want attention they hop on your lap. If they want to be left alone they run under the couch. And you know you're accepted if they do that cat "rearend in your face" greeting. I once read where that was a cat "acceptance signal," or "greeting." I'm just glad humans are more restrained in that department. I don't need to see Butch's butt to know he likes me.

Talk more. Express more. Engage in conversation more. It's not the other person's job. Remember, conversation is like a boat . . . when everyone is on one side, it sinks. It needs balance to stay afloat. Telling people how you feel is one of those things that gets lost in the rat race. "I'll do it tomorrow." "I'm sure they know."

I don't want to ruin my macho image, but every one of my conversations with my daughters ends with me saying, "I love you." I'm going to express that feeling until I draw my last breath. And every one of my conversations with my Mom ends with me saying, "I love you." Which always elicits her normal comeback . . . "Speak up, I can't read your mind." Mom's getting hard of hearing.

Chapter 33

You Share With Your Sister

· ·

Unselfishness

· ·

If ever there was a rule that would incur Mom's wrath, it was this one. My older sister and I were often paired up because of our closeness in age. We would get things, like games and candy, jointly. I grabbed all I could and inevitably heard, "Now you share with your sister." Hey, she had the same opportunity I did. Why should I be punished because I had better finger dexterity and could hold more M&M's or had better hand-eye coordination or could catch more candy thrown by Santa Claus during the Christmas parade. Not that the candy was any prize . . . it was rock hard. It made jawbreakers seem like cotton candy, and it tasted like swine feed. My apologies, I know this is an insult to the swine industry. Don't ask me how I know what swine feed tastes like. Here is an important candy rule: Except for Halloween, if it's free, it's because no one would buy it. If no one would buy it, how good can it be? If this stuff was sold, it would be sold in bulk — by the ton. But the deal here is that it was candy. Yee-haw! Free candy! Go get it! Go get all you can. Fill your pockets; fill those mittens on a string; take your sister's stocking cap off her head and fill it up.

Here's the odd thing . . . it's not that the candy was good. My sister and I called it "filling pullers." If you could chomp down on it, and you had a filling less than a month old, you'd yank that filling out. I didn't care that the candy was awful, I just wanted the candy — all I could get. This was probably the first sign I had obsessive-compulsive tendencies, and after the melee of fighting for the candy was over, I would hear Mom say, "Now you share with your sister."

Mom didn't want me to fall prey to the deadliest of sins . . . greed. Greed is wanting more than you need. Greed is wanting way too much. How much is too much? Well, having a house with an upstairs is enough, but having a house with something called "the west wing" is too much. Giving money to your alma mater, hoping they'll admit your child is enough, but giving so much money to your alma mater that your child ends up in a dorm with your name on it is too much. Having a closet full of clothes is enough, but having a closet closely resembling Macy's men's department including the escalator is too much.

That rule "now you share with your sister," is very ironic to me, because my older sister Gaylene, is one of the most unselfish people you'll ever meet. My first girlfriend was her best friend. . . how's that for sharing! Your welfare is more important to her than her own. Once when I was having a few bumps in my personal life, she wrote me a lengthy letter containing more wisdom on overcoming personal hardship than a year's worth of psychoanalysis. She could have just called or dropped me a card. I'm sure that would have taken much less time than carefully drafting that letter. But she didn't. I know she was busy but she still took time to share some thoughts with someone who needed it. Sharing is her lifestyle. Greed is not in her vocabulary.

Greed is such an easy thing to do. It's all around us. I'm not just talking about the athlete who is "insulted" by a 7-year, 90-million-dollar contract extension from the team who took a chance on him, groomed him, and nurtured him. I'm talking about all the little examples of greed that we experience every day. This is the kind of stuff that is just as dangerous as the headline-grabbing greed. I'm talking about the guy who takes the last four pillows from the overhead bin on the plane instead of just taking one. And what about that yapper at the check-out register that wants to be best friends with the clerk? It would be different if he or she were saving the world with deeds of humanity. Instead they're just talking about why that one guy on that one soap opera slept with that one gal. Or they're explaining the nuances of that gravy she makes every Thanksgiving that just drives her husband wild. Of course, *all* men are wild about gravy. Most men believe gravy is an entree. I think it was the gravy that made that one guy on the soap opera sleep with that one gal. Gravy can do that. Where was I? Oh, yeah. Yappers. And you're not one of those people who pokes every chocolate in the box to find the best one, are you? Or when you finish off the milk, do you put the empty jug back in the refrigerator? Do you squeeze 17 tomatoes before finding the one you like, leaving 17 bruised tomatoes for your fellow shoppers? And do you park on top of the white lines in the parking lot so you take up two spots?

And what do you do after you've found the number in the phone book or the yellow pages at the pay phone? Do you tear the entire page out of the book? After your wife gave birth Cesarean section did you complain about all of the time you wasted in natural childbirth classes?

Think about the other person a little bit. This is how we find happiness. Happiness is like a kiss, you must share it to have it. Charles Parkhurst said, "The man who lives by himself and for himself is likely to be corrupted by the company he keeps."

What is the devil inside us that starts making us think we are the only people out there. It probably is that buffet line. A buffet line where we just gorge ourselves holding a plate so big it takes two hands to hold it when it's *empty*. A dessert section with 14 selections and those are just the varieties of cheesecake. A side of beef so big the waiter is carving it with a chain saw. Some of these buffet lines are so long there's a rest stop at the halfway point. Gore, greed, glutton. Buffet lines are causing this. They are the root of all evil.

So why don't you give unselfishness a try. Don't share your views on religion and politics, and don't share your cold, but share pretty much everything else. Leave that last Kleenex in the box for the next person. Don't steal that pen in the bank by all the deposit slips. Save some toilet tissue on the roll. Pour that last bit of drink from the pitcher into your neighbor's glass, and let go with a couple of those french fries and just share with your sister.

Chapter 34

Put Cold Water On That Stain

• •

Urgency

• •

There's a genetic flaw in our family. We are sloppy eaters. This is how I know I am related to all of my relatives. Nature wins the debate over nurture. We are spread throughout the country and have been raised under different cultures, but we have one thing in common — we make a mess when we eat. The aftermath of a family reunion resembles that of a food fight. Never wear white at one of our family reunions because it won't be white for long. In fact, after one of our family dinners, if you see somebody in white, look closer, he's probably been hit with mayonnaise. Keeping your clothes clean at my family dinners is like running around in a shower to keep from getting wet. And if you think the adults are bad, you should see the kids. I can remember as a kid I'd know when dinner was over because the adults would get dessert and the kids would get hosed down.

When food was spilled on our clothes, it was a national emergency. Stains and spills and the fear of what they do have that effect on moms. It's like waving a red cape in front of a bull, or a Harvard pennant in front of a Yale man. Mom would bolt from her chair and say, "Quick, put some cold water on it . . . *now*!" That was the secret. Just put cold water on it and do it now. I don't know why Mom was so adamant about this. Those stains didn't seem to come out in the wash any better than those that hadn't been treated with cold water, but it didn't matter. Just put cold water on it — *now*.

I don't think Mom was as interested in teaching us laundry care as she was in teaching us urgency. There are some things in life where you stop what you're doing and take care of the urgent matter. Things like CPR, or the Heimlich maneuver. Things like answering the door when the Publisher's Clearing House Van is in the driveway, or stopping the car when that dash light flashes, "Check engine and call fire department." Or maybe patching things up with a relative before he goes to the Powerball headquarters with his winning ticket.

In time management seminars we learn that *urgent* projects take precedence over *important* projects. That may sound incorrect, but many times important projects don't have impending deadlines. They don't need to be attended to immediately. Do the urgent before you do the important. An urgent project is like a razor cut. When you nick yourself shaving, there is a sense of urgency to stop the bleeding *now*. You have to attend to it *now*, because despite what you learned in biology, all major arteries are near the surface of shaving areas. There is only one way to urgently fix this hemorrhaging aorta . . . you put a piece of Kleenex on it. Presto! You have taken care of an *urgent* problem and now you can continue to get dressed for work, an *important* project. The second urgent moment comes when you get to work and realize you forgot to remove the pieces of tissue. You've been walking around like abstract art while everyone laughs behind your back.

For most things though, we have little sense of urgency because we live in a world of procrastination. "Why do today what you can put off until tomorrow" is our motto. Now I'm not sure whether Mom ever had any bad experiences due to procrastination; I'm going ask her about that . . . one of these days . . . I just know you are either in the way or on your way, and I'm beginning to think that most people are in the way. There just doesn't seem to be any sense of urgency on anything anymore. Here's how you can tell if you've fallen into this trap:

- You don't pay any bill until the service is threatened to be shut off.
- You don't mow your grass until you receive hay baling bids from area farmers.
- You don't do laundry until you're down to those valentine boxer shorts that are two sizes too small.
- You don't go to the grocery store until you've eaten peanut butter and jelly sandwiches for nine straight meals.
- You don't get gas in your car until the light comes on that says, "Okay, idiot, you're on fumes!"

Now we don't have to treat everything like it's a national emergency, and I'm a little tired of those people who panic over the smallest of things, but some things do require urgency. Some issues require our immediate attention. Get off your lazy behind and get going. A hen is the only character that has produced noteworthy results from sitting down. Don't believe the old saying, "Everything comes to those who wait." The only things that come to people who wait are the next bus and lower back pain, so when in doubt, do something. Do it now! Stop telling your wife you're going to take her on a special vacation, call the travel agent. Quit borrowing your neighbor's saw, go to the hardware store and buy one. Stop saying you're going to take piano lessons, call the music teacher. Quit talking about cleaning the gutters, get out your ladder. Stop staring at that overgrown bush, find your hedge trimmers. And quit looking at that stain on your shirt and get some cold water on it, *now*.

Chapter 35

Put That Down, You Don't Know Where It's Been

•
Common Sense
•

I f you ever want a kid to pick up something or stick it in his mouth, just throw it on the floor. Really! You want kids to eat their vegetables, that's how to serve them. Call it "lima beans a la linoleum," or "carrots 'n carpet." Maybe it's because they're built closer to the ground; whatever the reason, if a kid sees something on the floor, two thoughts come to mind: *One,* pick it up; *two,* see what it tastes like. It's because of this, Mom, like every other mother, had to yell at us all the time, "Put that down, you don't know where it's been." This later became the rule, "Don't eat anything that's fallen on the floor." Your Mom may have had variations on this such as, "Don't eat anything that's still moving," or "Don't put anything in your mouth that's making a noise." Or "Don't be the second person to put the same thing in your mouth." Or, "Sharing is good, except for used gum." These all mean the same thing . . . put that down, you don't know where it's been.

The senses that propel a child to pick things up and use their mouth as a holding receptacle are the senses of sight, touch, taste, smell, and sometimes hearing. As a kid, those senses caused us to stick things in our mouths. How else would we ever know what dirt tastes like? But Mom wanted us to use our most valuable sense — common sense. Josh Billings said, "Common sense is instinct and enough of it is genius. It is the knack of seeing things as they are and doing things as they ought to be done." Unfortunately, common sense is very uncommon these days. It's about as common as a good hair day for Donald Trump.

I had a redneck buddy in high school who had a very simplistic quote: "If it makes sense, do it; if it don't make sense, don't do it — that's senseless." I always laughed at the blatant redundancy in that statement, but after watching some of the idiotic things we do in this country, I'm convinced we need to make it part of our daily mantra. This concept alone is how I would straighten out the problems with our judicial system — an entity sometimes completely void of common sense.

We give the difficult decision-making process to twelve people who aren't smart enough to get out of jury duty — that doesn't make sense. Don't do it, that's senseless. Give it to twelve people who are smart enough to digest information and make a reasonable judgment. Then pay them well for doing it. Why shouldn't jurors get paid well? Hey, society pays lawyers hundreds of thousands of dollars to try and get a guy off, and pays little to the twelve people who can actually do it. It's just common sense. Besides, what message is our current jury system sending to people? *"Mr. and Mrs. Juror, we want you to decide whether or not Mad Dog Magoon, who is charged with killing four people by repeatedly running them over with a rototiller, should be imprisoned or turned loose on society. To show you how important we think your job is, we're going to keep you away from your family for several months, make you eat every meal at Denny's, and pay you $6 a day."* No wonder most folks say jury duty ranks right up there with getting a root canal without Novocain.

I'm sick and tired of those legal beagles who twist and contort the law for the purpose of getting their obviously guilty clients acquitted. We need to give the judge the option of invoking a "common sense privilege." How would this work? Simple, let's take the case —a true story — of a man who savagely beat his girlfriend and stored her body in a trunk in his closet for 18 months. He flees the country while out on bail; is found guilty and sentenced to life imprisonment. Then he gets off because he was "tried in absentia" — a violation of his civil rights. That doesn't make sense. In *my* world, the judge would simply invoke the "common sense" privilege, and override the law. Why shouldn't judges invoke it? Parents all over the world use it every day. For example, you come into the kitchen and see your five year old with his mouth stuffed full of cookies and next to him is an overturned cookie jar — you don't dust the jar for prints or listen to your five year old's closing arguments. You declare him guilty as charged. Or your 18 year old comes home from the prom in the early morning hours, staggers into the bathroom, and positions his head over the commode. Who are the likely suspects for his condition? Bad broccoli or too much beer?

No cross-examination needed here. Another common-sense ruling is handed down (and the car keys taken away).

Cops make common sense rulings every day. They have to when they pull over someone who's just run a red light and the guy offers a lame excuse like, "I couldn't see the traffic signal officer, because there was a big red light shining in my eyes." Now I know many lawyers would argue that we must protect the fabric of the Constitution and every American's rights. However, I'm betting the framers' intent when they wrote the Constitution and the Bill of Rights wasn't so guilty people could walk free and imperil the lives of the innocent. I believe the ideals that Thomas Jefferson and the boys penned over 200 years ago are sacred. But I know they would roll over in their graves if they saw the all-inclusive way we have interpreted them. Don't tell me we can't change a word Tom and his friends wrote. Sure they were bright guys, but they weren't perfect. You've seen the pictures — they wore powdered wigs and pantyhose for heaven's sake. They believed in slavery and didn't think women should vote. Is it possible their opinion on other matters was subjective? We just need to ask the questions, "Does this make sense?" "Is it fair?"

I don't want to confine my lack of common sense bashing to the judicial system, though. This plague is everywhere. Can someone tell me why they ask that stupid question at the airports, "Did you pack your own bags?" Under what possible fantasy scenario would that stop a terrorist? I'm not sure, but I think they are likely to lie. Let me let you in on a secret: That investigative, high-security inquiry is not going to stop a terrorist. Do they really think he's going to say, "Aw shucks, I was hoping you wouldn't ask me that question, you got me. Handcuff me and take me in."

Ever wonder why most people don't buckle up in a car, but nearly everyone buckles up in the airplane? Let me ask a "common sense" question. If there was an accident, in which mode of transportation would a seat belt most likely help you? Think about it. I went through an emergency landing once on a commercial airline flight. In addition to the standard emergency procedures, they asked us to remove pens or any sharp objects from our pockets. Is this going to be my biggest worry? Most air crashes list people dying from impact or fire or smoke inhalation. How many passengers perish from pen impalement. The example that personifies this as much as any in recent history, though, is the lady who got pregnant despite using contraceptive jelly. She got pregnant because she put it on her toast. A news reporter asked her if she had read the instructions. Her response was succinct, "In a time of passion, you don't have time to read the instructions." Well, hello lady . . . you had time to make toast, maybe you had time to read those instructions.

So stop relying on those other senses so much, use that noggin a little more . . . if it don't make sense, don't do it—that's senseless. And put that down, you don't know where it's been.

Chapter 36

Go Pick Up Your Room

Unpleasantries

Teenager rooms are a disaster. Mine looked like a grenade hit it. Now, my daughters' rooms look the same way. Genetics did not take a holiday. If the governor saw my daughter's room he'd declare it a disaster. It looks like the place where celebrities urge, "For thirty cents a day, you can adopt this child." The thinking of my daughters is the same as my thinking. Why waste the time? If I'm going to put these clothes on in the next week, then there's no reason to waste the energy of picking them up, folding them, then putting them in the drawer. What a waste of time. They're perfectly comfortable right there. Leave them alone. They're resting. Go outside and do something productive with your time, like collecting caterpillars. That was always a fun thing to do as a kid.

Dirty rooms are a rite of passage. It's something we all must do. I remember one time looking in my closet and realizing that every single pair of jeans I owned was on the floor. It gave me a design idea for teenager bedrooms — no closets. Closets are a waste of space for teenagers. Remove the closet to create more floor space. That's what's needed. Give it that warehouse look. Then stuff could be neatly separated on the floor — easier to find. More efficient. More time. More caterpillars.

Lots of people think that rooms are dirty because teenagers are lazy. Wrong. The reason is because teens are the world's biggest believers in energy conservation. Especially when the energy they conserve is their own. Which is why they don't put things away, because they know they'll use them again, even if it's in the next decade. If everyone's room was like a teenager's, not only would we have no closets, we'd have no hangers, no chests or bureaus. Thus saving hundreds of thousands of acres of prime forest land, although I do realize it would cripple the furniture industry.

If the room is neat, someone must have vacuumed, which means you've been using up trees to make vacuum cleaner bags — you paper hog. What if comets and asteroids finally come crashing into Earth. Where would you rather be? In your mom's neat as a pin kitchen, or under three years' worth of clean laundry in your brother's bedroom.

There are other benefits in not cleaning your room that often go unnoticed. Pets prefer messy rooms over clean ones. Pets like to lay on stuff, and I don't mean linoleum. They like to rearrange, nest, and create the perfect bedding which they can only do if there is an assortment of socks, underwear, and shirts on the floor. The operative word is *assortment*, as in piles. Your parents may hate a trashed room, but your dog loves it. Who's your best friend anyway?

In an unkempt room, you would have a better picture of all your clothes, which will improve your fashion skills because you'll see what matches or clashes. You don't have to take clothes out of the closet and lay them next to each other to decide what to wear. It'll save time, which means, what? More caterpillars, of course. Although the teen fashions of today make wardrobe decisions quick and easy. *There are no rules!* But if your teenager does happen to ask what to wear with his T-shirt that says "Life Sucks," answer "wear it under a turtleneck."

Clothes on the floor eliminates those pesky decisions like: "Which drawer does this go in?" "Should I hang this or fold it?" "Should I put this with dress socks or casual socks?" These are the tough questions that shouldn't occupy the time of young people in their formative years. It's my belief that permanent emotional scars occur over the challenging questions I've posed.

Mom was a typical neat mother who was washing, mopping, scrubbing, and dusting anything that *didn't move*, which really irritated Grandpa. Let's face it, parents are supposed to be cleaner and neater. It's one of the mandatory differences between adolescents and adults. Just like facial hair. When I was a kid, my room wasn't going to be cleaner than my Aunt Myrtle's house, and I wasn't going to have more facial hair than her either. Just a fact of life. That's why I often tried to put off cleaning with smart aleck comments like, "Oh sure, Mom, I'll clean as soon as you rent me a bulldozer." Or, "Gee, Mom, I'm afraid to. There's stuff under my bed that's making a noise."

What reason do we have to expect kids to be neat. Think about it. For the first two years after a kid is born, what does he spend most of his time doing? Going to the bathroom without removing his pants. So why should we expect him to make picking up towels a priority? The question still is, "Where do kids learn to be so messy?" After all they're born naked, not in a pair of grungy sweats. Kids are born naked and clean, and immediately become dirty. And that's going to happen regardless of what Mom says.

I'm not so sure why the room had to be clean anyway? Did you ever hear your Mom say, "company's coming, so go make sure your room is picked up." First of all that doesn't make sense. How do you *pick up* your room? Who am I . . . Hercules? That's like the phrase "keep your ears open." What are the other options? Secondly, I never understood this clean room thing because Aunt Hazel never once walked into the house, put down her purse, and demanded to see my closet. That makes as much sense as, "company's coming, so let's make sure there's antifreeze in the Buick."

At some point, the conflict worsens and parents snap. Maybe it's when they find things in your room that they've been looking for — keys, clothes, your younger brother. Or they discover library books that were due three years ago. Parents snap and that's when cleaning your room becomes the basis of all goodness. Analogies are drawn that liken clean rooms to world peace. All evils in life are deeply rooted in dirty rooms.

If my Mom could have found headlines like these, I know she would have shoved them in my face. "Fulbright Scholarship Awarded to Local Student With Straight 'A' Average and Orderly Sock Drawer." Or, "Dr. Kevorkian Asked to End Misery of Parent Who Spent Seven Years Trying to Clean Teenager's Room."

Nothing is as important as a clean room. What if kids really believed that? Would your mother really want to have heard you say, "Mom, while you were out Publisher's

Clearinghouse Prize Patrol drove up and rang the doorbell and I said, 'No, you can't come in, I'm busy polishing the doorknob.'"

But parents aren't thinking straight when they reach that point. A clean room is the only thing that is important in their minds. It is a command of the highest order now. It is more than a simple request, and you know that if you're going to see your next birthday, you've got to clean the room.

There will always be things in life we don't want to do. As much as we dance around the issue, create excuses, find reasons to procrastinate, eventually we have to break down and do it. And I don't mean just do it to get it over with. I mean do it right. If you don't have time to do it right, do you really have time to do it over?

Whether it's cleaning your room, confronting your boss, writing that term paper, or remodeling the basement, eventually you can't avoid it any longer. That's when you acquiesce and accept the fact that life means sometimes doing things that are unpleasant.

The key to success doesn't always fit your ignition. But that's all right because adversity builds men and women. Maybe the greatest affliction of life, is never to be afflicted at all. Avoiding the tough things or dodging the issue may be fashionable, but not a mark of true winners. From time to time, you have to perform unpleasantries like cleaning your room. Do it and then go catch caterpillars.

Chapter 37

Pick Up Your Shoes

••••••••••••••••••••••••

Responsibility

••••••••••••••••••••••••

I have so much to say about shoes. First, it is one of the biggest differences between men and women. Men basically need a pair of dress shoes and a pair of tennis shoes. Women need a pair of dress shoes and a pair of tennis shoes for every color in the Sherwin Williams paint chart. Everyone assumed Imelda Marcos was the exception to the rule, but she was the norm. My daughters have shoe addictions and they'll never be cured. They have a mountain of shoes in the closet. If they don't have the time to find two that match in the pile, they just buy another pair. And how can they look at a closet filled with 87 pairs of shoes and say, "I don't have any shoes to wear with this outfit." Even Dennis Rodman could find a pair to his liking in that stack!

And why are there one inch heels, one-half inch heels, and three-quarter inch heels? Now how do you determine you're going to wear one of these sizes but not the others? How do you determine you need to be exactly one-quarter of an inch taller? I don't think you can blame this shoe business on the Garden of Eden. I'm not a theologian, but I'm pretty sure there's no reference to Eve demanding a pleasing pair of pumps.

And shoes can accumulate by the door. Walk in, kick them off, leave them by the door. The only place you don't see this is in soap operas. They always keep their shoes on. Ankle-breaking, arch-straining, toe-crunching shoes . . . and they never take them off. Normal people walk in the door and lose the shoes. Then they begin to accumulate. With a lot of kids in the family, this accumulation can be significant. In my family we couldn't have had more leather by the door if we'd shot a herd of cows as they broke in. You could see Mom beginning to get irritated as she would stumble across the pile or accidentally kick one across the room. And believe me, when you stumbled on my brother's 12D sneakers, you felt like you just tripped over a tire because his shoes had almost as much rubber as a Goodyear radial. Then Mom would blow. "Will you kids pick up your shoes! Why do I always have to tell you to pick up your shoes and put them away?" It wouldn't have bothered Mom if we had left our shoes there for a while, what irritated her was that we weren't responsible enough to put them up without being told. Mom was attempting to teach us responsibility.

Now there's a dying art — people being responsible without having a gun held to their head. Generally now we have to force responsibility. Responsibility just means doing what you're supposed to do without being told to do it. Like telling the truth, acting like an adult, and using good judgment if you're an elected official. I really didn't want to rant on this but I just can't resist.

There's not enough space here to write about all the irresponsible actions of elected and appointed officials over the past few years. Where would I begin? We've had a President getting sexual favors in the Oval office, a Governor trying to sell a Senate seat, a Congressman sending nude pictures of himself on the Internet, Judges taking cash, and I haven't even touched the surface. Some people want to give them a pass because they've served their people so well. Sorry, gotta hit the buzzer on that one. A few years of highly compensated pay doesn't give someone a pass for totally irresponsible behavior. And that's what it is plain and simple. They were elected or appointed to be a LEADER first and foremost. It's a breach of contract in my mind.

And one more thing. It *does* say something about their ability to perform the job. Their job is to make decisions, often very tough decisions. Those types of egregious actions I've just mentioned obviously show poor judgment. In other words, bad decision making skills. It's pretty easy to connect the dots. They're incompetent to perform the job. They need to go away.

Here's the real irony. What many of these folks have done would have got you or I fired from any job we had. Or if your kid would have done it, you'd have grounded them until they could draw Social Security. Yet there's still a lot of people that hold them to a *lower* standard and want them to stay on the job. Weird.

Speaking of weird, that wasn't a very funny piece of writing was it? I know, but allow me this one hot button rant. It was on one of my favorite subjects: responsibility.

Winston Churchill said, "Responsibility is the price of greatness." We live in the greatest country with the greatest system, but that comes with a price: responsibility. We have to pick up the pace a little when it comes to being responsible. And while we're at it, pick up our shoes too. It's the responsible thing to do. So says my mom.

Chapter 38

If You Can't Say Something Nice, Then Don't Say Anything At All

•••••••••••••••••••••••••

Tolerance

•••••••••••••••••••••••••

It was Mom's house and she didn't allow bad talk. Many times I can remember griping about something or somebody and then hearing, "If you can't say something nice, then don't say anything at all." Of course, today if you can't say something nice, you've probably got your own radio talk show. But when I was a kid Mom didn't want us to become one of those intolerant old gruffs that every family has. You know who I'm talking about. The person who always finds the negative to everything. You tell them it's a beautiful day outside, they say, "It means there's a nasty one around the corner." You tell them those are beautiful roses and they say, "It's a shame they die so dang quickly." These people have a constant scowl on their faces and they look like they were weaned on lemon juice. It used to be that there were only a few people out there with that chip on their shoulder griping about everything, but they've multiplied. We've got intolerant gruffs lurking around every corner and they're as unhappy as Bob Vila's neighbor trying to sleep in.

Now if you've driven 15 miles to attend your stress reduction class and they lost your registration, I know you have a right to be upset, but overall, what's the big deal? Why can't we be more tolerant? We live better, we eat better, we live longer, we work less, we have remote control. How can we be so intolerant of people and little bumps in the road? Ken McFarland, my mentor from my hometown and one of the great motivational speakers of all time, told of running into one of these intolerant gruffs. McFarland said, "Good morning," and this gentleman said, "What's so good about it?" McFarland's response was simple, "Try missing one." Gripe, gripe, gripe. My coffee is too hot. My coffee is too cold. This doesn't taste right. Why did that letter take three days to get here? We need to be more tolerant and more understanding. If your first reaction is to snap somebody's head off, take a break, count to ten, put a bucket of ice in your shorts, cool off, calm down, and say something nice.

If you're in the checkout line at the supermarket and a guy taps you on the shoulder and says, "Please, I've only got this one item, can I go ahead of you?" And you say, "Certainly, my good man, obviously you need to suck down that six-pack of BelchMore beer quicker than my infant needs this high-protein formula." Then you need to be a little more tolerant. If you're stuck in a traffic jam so long that your tie goes out of and back into style and meanwhile the ignoramus in the car right behind you is laying on his horn like he's rehearsing for a jazz band, and then you walk back to him and say, "Thanks for keeping me alert to the fact that in the last 30 minutes I've moved about as far as a Greenland ice glacier," then you need to be more tolerant.

Over coffee one time I heard a woman say, "Why would anybody want to win that $34 million Power Ball? Do you realize how much you'd have to pay in taxes?" Often people who can't say something nice are not very intelligent people, so if you can't say something nice, then just don't say anything at all. Save all of us the grief.

Our tolerance is tested, though, every day. That's why they created Barney. That's an adult tolerance test. If you can watch him for 20 minutes without throwing the remote at the TV, you pass. If you can stay in a good mood despite having that "I love you song" in your head all day long, you pass (right now you're probably singing that song and hating me for bringing it up).

I was having work done on my car recently and was in the waiting area at the car dealership when a mother and her small child turned the TV to the Barney guy. It was a test. I didn't do well. I had to go into the shop. I helped rotate the tires and change a timing belt. I prefer mechanic work to purple dinosaurs. But I understand that my television tastes are different than a child's television interests (my Mother disagrees with me here), and I try to be tolerant of the kids.

And I've noticed something over time. There seems to be a connection between tolerance and gossip. People who aren't very tolerant are excellent at gossip, and gossip is very popular these days. I swear more people are run down by gossip than by automobiles. I always remember what my favorite and most impressionable teacher, Ralph Field, used to say: "Great people talk about ideas, good people talk about things, and little people talk about other people." Here's a test you can take. If you got $1 for every kind word you said, but had to pay $10 for every unkind word you said, would you be rich or poor? Gossipers would be poor because most gossip is negative and is intolerant.

So how tolerant are you? Do you go ballistic when the Happy Meal has the wrong Beanie Baby in it? Do you make terrorist's threats if you can't get an aisle seat on the plane? Do you threaten sterilization to the cable guy if he's late? We're constantly faced with tolerance tests. Like with your teenager's music. I know I'm sounding like my Dad here, but I'd rather listen to Lawrence Welk at half speed than a lot of today's top ten hits. Or like dinner with your elderly relatives: Look Aunt Rose, I'm sorry you don't feel well, but I don't need to hear such detail about your foot fungus, especially while I'm eating sponge cake. This is how I feel, but I'm not going to say anything. I am going to ease up a bit. I'm going to be more tolerant.

Do you give a little, or are you as rigid as a professional sports union executive? We need to start looking for the good in someone, seeing what's right with the situation, finding the positive in the disappointment, and be more tolerant of our fellow man and woman. If you can't say something nice about someone, then don't say anything at all . . . unless, of course, it happens to be Barney — he's fair game.

Chapter 39

Never Talk To Strangers

•••••••••••••••••••••••••

Caution

•••••••••••••••••••••••••

This was always a difficult rule to follow. Mom didn't want us talking to strangers for the obvious reason the world has a few perverts and crackpots so warped you can't predict what they may do. When I was a kid, though, strange meant you were known to put catsup on everything including your oatmeal; or you were still wearing your letter jacket at age 46. Strange today, however, means . . . *strange*. If I had followed that rule to the letter I would never have spoken to half my relatives. Some of them I never saw except for once every two years. I couldn't pick them out of a lineup, I mean a crowd. I don't want you to think I dislike my relatives, it's just that put them all together and they make the "Addams Family" look like the "Brady Bunch." Many of my relatives were complete strangers to me. And you had to see some of my relatives. I had uncles who could grow facial hair out of every orifice on their heads like Rogaine on steroids. How was it okay to talk to a stranger (who had what looked like a ferret growing out of his nose) at a family gathering, but it wasn't okay to talk to the guy in the grocery store handing out candy. This was very confusing for a little kid.

Of course, Mom was just trying to teach us caution. We could use that in many facets of life. Use a little caution on those decisions like when you're choosing a physician, select-ing a school, or investing your life savings. No need to bolt to a quick decision and throw caution to the wind. Here are some of life's cautionary tips:

1) Don't take investment tips from anyone with a one-word name, i.e., Lefty, Lucky, or Slick.

2) Don't hire a KISS band member as your cosmetic counselor.

3) Don't ask a barber if he thinks you need a haircut.

4) Don't have your taxes done by a guy working out of the back seat of a Pinto.

5) Don't accept that the used car you're buying never had an identification number.

6) Don't ever sign a surgical release from a door-to-door liposuction salesman.

7) Never eat anything at a taxidermist's house that you can't identify.

8) Never buy an automobile transmission in kit form.

We just need to be more cautious, prudent and safe. Oh, what the heck, you say, sometimes you have to take a risk.

I agree, but risk putting on a pound by eating that double-fudge-chocolate-brownie-caramel-nut dessert, don't risk your entire future on a an "iffy" business opportunity. Risk losing your appetite by riding that thrill-a-second, hair-raising, heart-stopping roller coaster, but don't risk your life being stupid on the highway. Remember, a good risk gets your heart pumping, a bad risk could stop it. A good financial risk can double your bank account, a bad risk can empty it.

Being a little more cautious might slow down this body piercing phenomenon. How ridiculous has this become? I can understand the ear piercing, and can even understand the belly button thing, but why are people piercing eyebrows, lips, tongues, noses, and private parts that only Howard Stern talks about? It's common knowledge that all living organisms have two basic functions: To eat and reproduce. This body piercing interferes with these two basic instincts. It's not right and it's not safe. I saw someone the other day with both their nose and ear pierced and the piercings were connected with a gold chain. How healthy is this? A runny nose could spread into an ear infection in no time. Please, people, be more cautious.

We can still satisfy that need for excitement in our life without being . . . uh . . . being . . . uh . . . okay, stupid! We've all done stupid things. Afterwards, we said those infamous words, "What was I thinking?" And the answer, of course, is nothing. Now while it's true, you're being way too cautious if you wait four hours to go swimming after eating a cup of low-fat yogurt, or if you look both ways before crossing your living room, or if you refuse to give your Social Security number over the phone . . . to your mother. I'm not saying that you should be that cautious. You can be too cautious and take the excitement out of your life. But I'm saying, "Be smart about it." It's exciting to prepare, train, and climb a mountain, it's dumb to do it on a dare. It's exciting to plan something special for your anniversary, it's dumb not to include your wife. It's okay to be a free spirit and fire from the hip occasionally, but big decisions in life require caution. Be careful! I had a friend who used to say, "Drive in such a manner that your license will expire before you do." We must act with conviction, but we must deliberate our actions with caution. So use some of that caution when that guy tries to get you to invest in his combination outdoor grill-riding lawn mower invention. He could be your long-lost, hair-tufts-in-the-ear Uncle Arnold. Don't talk to him. He's **strange**!

Chapter 40

Go To Your Room Until You Stop Crying

....
Sanctuaries
....

W e've all been sent to our rooms for crying. No two ways about it — crying is one of the most annoying things you can do to parents. Think of the last airline flight you had where the baby cried the entire flight. It was probably compounded by the tray table police serving food you couldn't give away in Ethiopia, and the Sumo wrestler wedged in next to you who got in and out of his seat five times before takeoff. I'll bet you had a headache after a while. You probably wanted to volunteer to help that crying child — if you know what I mean.

Even the most tolerant parent will eventually reach the boiling point and resort to the last draw. "Go to your room until you stop that crying." Or, how about: "Stop that crying or I'll give you something to cry about!" Mom, I already have a reason; if you want me to cry about something else, take a number. And what was Mom going to do to make me cry more? Tell me bad news? — Flipper is allergic to water? My friend, Flicka, had been sent to the glue factory?

Mom wanted me to go to my room until I stopped crying, and that always seemed a bit odd. Did she think I was going to feel any better in my room. But, you know what, she was right. After a while I would indulge myself in a puzzle, or draw on my Etch-A-Sketch, or play with my army men. And stop crying. That room was my sanctuary, a place I could go and get away from it all.

Of course today, sending a kid to his or her room might not be punishment, not when the average kid's room has a television, a telephone, a boom box, and a computer. I'm not sure how you update that rule about crying in today's world. "Go to your room until you stop crying and don't even think of getting on line or watching MTV."

Whether or not we are crying, we need a sanctuary from our stressors. Someplace to go and get away. I have two sanctuaries: airplanes and hotels. That may seem unusual, but this is how I've learned to handle the rigors of travel. When I'm in those two settings, I'm in my own little world. This is why I'm not a very good conversationalist on the airplane. I don't want to carry on a two-hour conversation with someone who wants to be my best friend. I give them obvious hints: I read and sleep. If that doesn't work, I start pulling out tricks, like making a hand puppet out of the air-sick bag, or playing the drum solo from "Wipe Out" on my tray table, or spending the flight slurping every last ounce from my carry-on colossal Big Gulp. If they are still pestering me, I bring out my emergency plan: "I'd like to offer you the opportunity to invest in a multi-level marketing program." Or, "Let me share with you what I learned in prison." These people don't understand that this is my sanctuary. I want to read or sleep, in other words, I want to be left alone. So just in case you're ever sitting next to me on a plane, let's get some things straight right now. Spare me the details of your dumb brother-in-law's investment in a Mazola oil well. And, no, I don't think the man in 17D looks like Willy Wonka.

When I was in college I found a jogging partner in Father Karl Kramer. He was the Catholic priest at the St. Isidore's Parish in Manhattan, Kansas. I needed a running partner because without one I would cheat. I would slow down, take shortcuts, or just stay in bed and tell everyone I ran six miles. At first I thought Father Kramer was a cream puff because he was 5'4", weighed barely 100 pounds, and was 56 years old. But he nearly killed me. The first morning we ran together we did 10 miles. At the end of the run he said, "I'll see you in the morning." I said, "Are you coming by the hospital?" In two weeks I managed to get some arch back in my right foot and met Father Kramer for another run. I asked him how often he did this and he said he ran every day regardless of the weather. He said this was his "non-religious sanctuary," a place where he could get away and clear his mind.

We all need sanctuaries, whether it's a chalet in France or a jogging route in our home town, we all need a place to get away. My other sanctuary is a hotel room. I seldom explore a city when I'm on business traveling. I order a fruit plate, hibernate, catch up on the news, watch a movie, and avoid contact with the human race. My kids are like me too — they love hotels and they love room service. For a kid this is cool.

Order food on the phone, eat in your room, and leave the mess behind. Please, don't try this at home.

Once when my girls were younger, we were at a resort that allowed guests to order breakfast the night before by placing an order on the doorknob. We couldn't agree on anything, so every box on the order form was marked: milk, orange juice, hot chocolate, bacon, ham, sausage, toast, pastries . . . and since we all wanted two eggs, we ordered six eggs. I assumed there would be a place to request a number of place settings, so I told my daughter to mark "3" since there were three of us. The problem is that it didn't ask for the number of settings, it asked for the number of servings. The next morning the man from room service showed up with three of everything, plus 18 eggs. Room service cost me $115 and this was 1985. The room service guy wanted to know if we were expecting company. The girls thought we couldn't go play until all the food was gone.

Hotels are my get-a-way, and that's why I hate to be disturbed. Apparently, in many foreign languages, "Do Not Disturb," means "barge in with a vacuum cleaner while they're naked." And I don't need turn-down service at 9:00 p.m. How did turn-down service get started? Did someone call the front desk and say, "Uh, this is Mr. Mayfield in 311; say, this bed I've got here, how, how do you get into it?"

While I'm at it, when are hotels going to come up with some services we can really use? Like one standardized, universal shower control. You never know if turning that knob to the left is going to give you cold water or water hot enough to melt your shampoo bottle. Why don't the light switches in the hotel rooms make sense? Why should I have to turn the shower light on to get the TV to work? But despite all of these irritations, my hotel room is my sanctuary. It's where I escape to.

What is your get-a-way option to stop you from "crying"? Is it a place of solitude? Henry David Thoreau said, " I never found a companion that was so companionable as solitude." Do you have someplace to go? My sanctuary used to be the kitchen. I would unwind by drinking a glass of milk and eating a box of animal crackers. It was a ritual. Then one evening I read on the box, "do not eat if seal is broken." The giraffe appeared to be okay and the bear was only missing one claw, but the seal was all smashed up. I began to cry. Mom said "go to your room" and all of a sudden I found a new sanctuary. Where is yours? The next time you're upset or depressed or stressed out, you know what to do — go to your room. I bet you'll stop crying.